I0088059

From This Day Forward

Preparing
Couples
for the
Journey of a Lifetime

Couple's Edition

Dr. Michael J. Peck

All Scripture quotations are from the Authorized King James Version of the Holy Bible.

ISBN 978-1-936285-02-0

Published by Baptist Church Planters
36830 Royalton Road
Grafton, Ohio 44044

440-748-1677

Web Site: www.bcpusa.org
Email: bcp@bcpusa.org

Designed by an idea—anideaweb.com

A Word from the Author

From This Day Forward—Preparing Couples for the Journey of a Lifetime is a premarital manual more than three decades in the making. Before coming to Baptist Church Planters, it was my privilege to serve as the pastor of several wonderful Baptist churches in New York. During those thirty-one years, many couples sat in my office, and together we prepared for their coming wedding.

In every sense of the word, marriage is a journey of a lifetime. There will be times of joy, blessings, surprises, and growth. Along the journey of a lifetime, there will also be adjustments, trials, and even some times of sorrow. Every day brings new opportunities to trust the Lord and grow in your love for your mate.

Prepare well for this journey. Each counseling session you invest with your future mate and pastor will help you to become the husband or wife God wants you to be. As you read the various chapters and complete the homework assignments, view them as a welcome opportunity to strengthen your future marriage and home. While grandchildren may be far from your mind at the present, in a very real sense, what you are doing now in your engagement and marriage is preparing the way for the next generations in your family.

May the Lord richly bless you and your future mate as you prepare for the journey of a lifetime.

"Through wisdom is an house builded;

and by understanding it is established:

And by knowledge shall the chambers be filled

with all precious and pleasant riches."

(Proverbs 24:3-4)

Acknowledgements

A very special thank you goes to my dear wife Karen. She is my best friend. Her faithful walk with the Lord, her love for me, and her commitment to our marriage make writing a premarital counseling handbook not only possible, but a joy.

Many staff partners carefully and prayerfully helped me with the manuscript production. They have a great eye for details, and I am grateful to the Lord for their investment of time and effort.

To my friend and editor, Robert Bowker, a sincere thank you is extended. His contribution to the book is hard to describe. Bob's expertise in editing is invaluable, and his suggestions are excellent. You are a faithful partner in ministry, Bob.

To my friend, Lawrence Montgomery, thank you for the hours you invested on the manuscript. Your suggestions are so appreciated.

Lastly, thank you to my family and friends who kept praying and encouraging me to write this handbook. Your partnership continues to be an incredible blessing. You will never know how much your prayers have helped me in this project.

Contents

From This Day Forward
Preparing Couples for the Journey of a Lifetime

Getting the Most from Your Premarital Counseling

Congratulations! What an exciting time you have arrived at in your lives! As the bride and groom you face days of anticipation, excitement, a number of details that threaten to overwhelm you, and of course, the sheer joy of knowing you will soon be married.

Though my wedding day took place many years ago, I remember it as if it were yesterday. My wife Karen and I were married in my junior year in Bible College. She willingly worked full-time and I continued full-time studies and a part-time student pastorate. We lived in a two-room apartment on a very small income. Though we had little of this world's goods, we were so blessed! With two very different personalities and two very different backgrounds, we were (and still are!) deeply in love and joyfully married.

The handbook you hold, *From This Day Forward,* is a combination of spiritual principles and practical applications from our personal marriage and my pastoral practice. Today, my wife Karen and I are the very best of friends. Daily we thank the Lord for the wonderful marriage He continues to nurture in our lives. I can guarantee that the Lord greatly desires to do the same thing for you.

You are about to start a series of counseling sessions aimed at preparing you for marriage. To get the very most out of your time with the counseling pastor, you must commit to several things:

1. As the bride and groom, you must commit to pleasing the Lord. Colossians 1:10 provides both a motive (*"That ye might walk worthy of the Lord unto all pleasing"*) as well as a method (*"Being fruitful in every good work, and increasing in the knowledge of God"*) that will help guide

you as a couple. Personally apply the motive (pleasing God) and the method (being fruitful and increasing in the knowledge of God) as dynamics that will help you to begin well the journey of a lifetime.

2. Together, you both must commit to taking seriously the weeks of premarital counseling. Your commitment will be demonstrated in two ways: first by your attitude, and secondly by your actions. An attitude of being teachable and a willingness to learn, as well as actions of commitment to completing the homework and finishing the tests, are absolutely essential.

3. Another commitment you both must make and keep is to take extra precautions of moral purity during this very special time of your lives. The weeks and months before your wedding will be a period of time in which you will face the greatest temptations to let down your guard morally. The enemy and destroyer of marriages will whisper something like, "Go ahead-you are going to be married soon anyway. Everyone else enjoys intimacy ahead of time. You should have a little fun as well. It will be exciting. Don't wait!" If you have waited, keep waiting until after your wedding. You will both be glad you made this choice. The groom must be the spiritual leader and protect their relationship, especially in this area.

If you have been sexually active, now is the time to commit to abstinence from this day until your wedding night. You cannot go back and relive your life. However, you can determine that, from this day forward, your goal will be to please the Lord. It will not be possible to please the Lord if you are deliberately doing something that He has forbidden.

God has given married couples a wonderful gift. The writer of Hebrews declared, *"Marriage is honorable in all, and the bed undefiled"* (13:4). Be assured, the excitement of intimacy and sexual pleasure within the bonds of marriage awaits you. Be on guard right now! Set clearly-established limits of affection and deliberately seek to honor the Lord and each other by your commitment to moral purity.

4. Your pastor-counselor will assign homework and various tests throughout the counseling process. You will find the appropriate homework and test at the beginning of each session. Notice that the sessions will include tests for both the bride and the groom. Unless your counselor specifically tells you to take the test together, all tests should be completed separately. Do not discuss the answers with each other ahead of time unless otherwise directed.

Your counselor may direct you to remove the tests from your handbook, or he may give you special instructions for making copies of your test answers. The advantage of copying your test answers is that your book remains intact as a keepsake of your wedding. Do your best to comply with his directions. The groom and bride should work only in his or her handbook.

5. Come to your counseling appointments with this handbook, a pen, your Bible, and an eagerness to invest in your future marriage. Space will be provided in each chapter for you to take notes during the session. Enter into the counseling sessions with great expectations that the Lord has brought you and your future mate to a great journey that will last a lifetime. Right now He desires to help and prepare you for this wonderful journey together.

Read through each chapter carefully and thoughtfully. May the Lord greatly bless you in every way as you look forward to your wedding and married life together.

"No Longer Alone—Praise the Lord!"

No longer alone! Together we go hand in hand,

Trusting the Lord completely. His will we want to understand.

His blessings are precious. He truly is great.

God's very best is our desire in the marriage He will create.

"My beloved is mine, and I am his" (Song of Solomon 2:16).

Information Intake—*Introducing ourselves*

Bride's Information:

Bride's full name _____

Address _____

Date of birth _____ Home phone _____

Cell phone _____

Status: Is this your first marriage? _____

Are you a member of a local church? _____

Name of church _____

Family background:

Names of parents _____

Names and ages of siblings _____

_____

Do you have a personal relationship with the Lord Jesus Christ?_____

If yes, please write a brief paragraph of your testimony of salvation. _____

_____

_____

_____

What are several of the goals for premarital counseling you wish the pastor to emphasize?_____

_____

Are you committed to six (may vary) sessions of premarital counseling and the completion of homework assignments before each appointment?

_____

Date of proposed wedding _____

Location of proposed wedding _____

Groom's Information:

Groom's full name _____

Address _____

Date of birth _____ Home phone _____

Cell phone _____

Status: Is this your first marriage? _____

Are you a member of a local church? _____

Name of church _____

Family background:

Names of parents _____

Names and ages of siblings _____

_____

Do you have a personal relationship with the Lord Jesus Christ? _____

If yes, please write a brief paragraph of your testimony of salvation. _____

_____

_____

_____

What are several of the goals for premarital counseling you wish the pastor to emphasize? _____

_____

Are you committed to six (may vary) sessions of premarital counseling and the completion of homework assignments before each appointment?

_____

Foundations for Every Couple

Perhaps this is the first time you have ever made an appointment with your pastor for counseling. As the appointment approaches, many couples discover a mix of emotions ranging from excitement to a little apprehension. Rest assured—your pastor is most pleased to invest this time in your lives. He is a man called of God to shepherd the Lord's people. As a shepherd, your pastor really cares about you as a couple and desires the Lord's very best for your lives.

Do not hesitate to be very honest and truthful with your future mate and your pastor. While heeding the Apostle Paul's caution to be *"Speaking the truth in love"* (Ephesians 4:15), understand that these months are some of the most important times in your life. You are preparing for a lifetime journey. Your pastor will not be shocked at anything you share with him. Doubtless he has heard it many times before. Be encouraged to make the premarital counseling experience profitable and an enriching time of spiritual and emotional growth.

Work on this section before your counseling session

Take a few moments to read Genesis 2:18-24. You are reading the account of the first wedding ceremony. Think about several key elements from the Scripture.

Why do you think God said, *"It is not good that the man should be alone?"*

_____

_____

What is the significance of the Lord's statement, "I will make him an help meet for him?" (The word "meet" has to do with "fitting just right.")

_____

_____

How does your future mate fill the role of "help meet" in your personal life? _____

Your future mate should have a very special place in your heart as "help meet." How do you communicate this to him or her?

_____

_____

Have you ever considered putting your thoughts in writing to express your love and appreciation to your future mate for being your "help meet?" Some find writing to be very difficult. Whenever it is possible, even a brief note that expresses such appreciation may become a keepsake on your journey. You may use the margin to draft your note.

In what ways are you a "help meet" for your future mate? _____

_____

Are you unsure about this biblical role of being a "help meet?" If so, would you be willing to discuss it with your future mate and, if necessary, with your counseling pastor? Make yourself open and vulnerable by being honest with your questions.

Think about the Essential Elements of Successful Marriage

There are several key elements that are absolutely essential in laying a great foundation for your marriage. What an exciting time this is! To successfully map a loving relationship on the journey of your lifetime, be sure to incorporate each of these key principles into your marriage.

1. I must have the sweet confidence that this is the will of God for us.

Psalm 40:8, *"I delight to do thy will, O my God,"* is a reminder to you both that the Lord has a plan for your lives. Your pastor will be very interested in learning how you as a couple have arrived at the decision that this marriage is the will of God for you.

Sometimes couples marry for all the wrong reasons. What would you list as several wrong reasons for getting married? _____

_____

2. I must have the personal desire to marry this person.

You are soon to marry and will be able to identify with the situation Rebekah was facing. Was she truly willing to marry Isaac? Genesis 24:58 states, *"And they called Rebekah and said unto her, Wilt thou go with this man? And she said, I will go."*

No one should be pressuring you. Are you entering into this wedding and marriage of your own voluntary decision and will? If you are struggling in this area, you must ask the Lord to give you the courage and graciousness to talk with your future mate and pastor about this.

3. I must view marriage properly as a lasting pledge or covenant.

The Lord Jesus declared, *"Wherefore they are no more twain, but one flesh. What therefore God hath joined together, let not man put asunder"* (Matthew 19:6).

This really is, "For better or worse…as long as life shall last." Divorce is a word that must be discarded, and NEVER entertained as an option. The picture of God joining couples together and no man ever putting them asunder is glorious and delightful as the years roll along.

4. I must make the daily consistent investment.

The Apostle Paul expressed it this way, *"Submitting yourselves one to another in the fear of God"* (Ephesians 5:21).

Daily it is important to remember you no longer have ownership rights to your life. You have permanently and powerfully given yourself to another. Likewise, your future mate joyfully gives himself or herself to you in an ongoing act of mutual submission. Each living for the other requires a consistent investment of the heart, and life. Demanding? Yes, but well worth every bit of effort.

Work on this section during your counseling session

Your pastor will share with you at least seven reasons that premarital counseling is so important. As you fill in the blanks, think of how these statements relate to you and your future mate.

The Importance of Biblical Premarital Counseling

There are many good reasons to commit to premarital counseling. Here are several such reasons.

1. Your wedding will be one of the most significant days in your entire life. Premarital counseling is going to _____

   _____.

   Marriage is too important to enter into without good preparation. Ask the Lord to give you an excitement and determination as you enter these sessions.

2. The premarital counseling process will assist you as a couple to

   _____

   relationship with each other. Do not settle for mediocrity in your marriage!

3. The premarital counseling time will enable _____

   _____

   to enrich the engagement season for you and your future mate.

4. As a couple, this time of counseling will help you to _____

   _____

   before the wedding. You may already be aware of several situations that need to be addressed or changed. It is not wise to assume that problem situations will automatically change after the wedding.

Never assume you will be able to change another person. Only the Holy Spirit can change people. Wise couples learn to be honest in their view of self, each other, and their relationship. Strengths that complement, as well as weaknesses that may potentially harm the relationship, are better dealt with now than later. Many adjustments, some of which are wonderful, lie ahead. Seeking the Lord's help and applying biblical counsel will afford you as a couple the great joy of change and becoming more like the Lord Jesus.

5. Carefully and honestly working through the premarital counseling process will help _____

_____

after the wedding.

6. As a couple, you are busy. However, the time invested together with your counselor will provide the opportunity to _____

_____

questions. You have never traveled this road before. Your pastor brings rich ministry to you. He is a man with training, preparation, and personal experience. Across the room from you is seated a man who will be a great source of information and counsel.

7. Always, the Lord Jesus _____

_____

as a believer. The days before your wedding will be some of the most significant days of your lifetime. What better time is there to honestly evaluate your personal spiritual condition? Becoming a committed, thoroughly-devoted disciple of the Lord Jesus Christ will make you a far better husband or wife. Throughout your counseling time, there will be many opportunities to make decisions which will cause you to grow spiritually.

Four Principles to Insure a Strong Biblical Foundation

Your counselor will share with you and your future mate four very practical and powerful principles from the marriage of Adam and Eve. Take careful notes, because the strength of your marriage depends upon the personal application of these principles.

My Personal Notes from this Counseling Session

_____

_____

_____

_____

While these four principles may not be the norm today, they are nevertheless God's plan for a successful marriage. The Lord, who created and designed the husband and wife relationship, clearly reveals what makes marriages work. Are these the goals you wish to establish on your journey of a lifetime?

1. Be sure to ask the pastor any questions that may have surfaced today. Do not think any question is insignificant or silly.

2. The pastor will assign the homework entitled "Respect and Priority." Check with him as to when this homework is due. With his permission, you may wish to make copies of your homework rather than tear the pages from your handbook so you will have your notes intact as a keepsake of your wedding.

3. Some pastors may wish to schedule the next counseling session at this time. Others prefer to schedule it after you submit your next homework assignment.

Ask the Lord to make these well-known principles real to both you and your future mate. The Lord Jesus reminds His disciples, "If you know these things, happy are ye if ye do them" (John 13:17). There is a huge difference between knowing and doing!

"How Greatly I am Blessed"

I am blessed indeed by our gracious Lord!

He truly leads me through His precious Word.

I am not left alone to make decisions today;

Before His throne I can humbly pray.

Lord, You are wonderful—so good you are to me.

I'm so glad to be part of Your precious family.

So, daily I will trust You and grow in Your grace.

Make my life a blessing in this lifelong race.

Let the Journey Begin!

Respect is the communication of appreciation that you have for your future mate. Priority is the demonstration of what is important to you. Both respect and priority are essential to healthy marriages. Do you and your future mate respect each other? Are you demonstrating that your future partner is a great priority in your life?

Work on this section before your counseling session

Your answers to questions 1-6, found after the story of Mark and Mindy, should be copied and given to the pastor before your next counseling session.

"Respect and Priority"

Name _____

The Story of Mark and Mindy

Mark and Mindy arrived for their premarital counseling appointment with nervousness and anticipation. They were to be married in less than six months and this would potentially be one of the most important moments in their lives.

Mark grew up in a home where fighting and friction became part of daily living. Neither of Mark's parents are believers and both mom and dad were demanding and self-centered. While the fighting seldom was physical, the emotional damage was severe. Mark's mother never worked outside the home. She views her husband as a failure who never measured up to her expectations. Often she would complain that they needed more money. Mark's dad became more and more withdrawn and seemed to find his fulfillment through his work. He worked more hours, came home less frequently and though they made more money, the home became more tense and unhappy. They divorced each other four years before Mark and Mindy became engaged.

Everyone in Mindy's family is a believer. Her mom is a career woman. She has taught in the same elementary school since she graduated from college. Dad owns and operates his own business. Both are supportive of each other's careers. Both are very active in their local church. Mom teaches children, and dad is an usher and treasurer. Mom is a conversationalist and very much wants to talk with her husband about everything. She teases him that after spending all day with third graders, she would like to talk with an adult. Dad is a very gracious man and often compliments his wife. They love to talk with each other, and are faithful in their devotions. Their home, while not perfect, is warm, loving, respectful and spiritually minded.

This is the background of Mark and Mindy. Based on this information, in your own words, please answer the following questions.

1. Knowing that our values and impression of marriage are caught from watching our parents, how would you express the most likely picture Mark and Mindy have when it comes to marriage?

   Mark's picture: _____

   _____

   Mindy's picture: _____

   _____

2. What were the obvious priorities in the families of both Mark and Mindy?

   Mark's family: _____

   _____

Mindy's family: _____

_____

3. How would you counsel Mark and Mindy concerning the right priorities to begin establishing in their marriage, based on their pictures?

_____

_____

4. How were respect and priority communicated in the home in which you grew up? _____

_____

5. What are the ways your future mate communicates respect and priority to you? _____

_____

_____

_____

6. How do you communicate respect and priority to your future mate?

_____

In this counseling session, you will be discussing with your counselor the importance of communicating respect and priority to your future mate. *Respect* is the recognition of who your future mate is as a person. This speaks of honoring the character and reputation of your future mate. *Priority* is the place your future mate holds in your life as well as the importance you assign to your marriage. The answers to your homework will assist your counselor in this session.

You may be surprised to learn of the comparison of your future marriage to a beautiful lawn or a healthy bank account. The comparisons are many. Lawns that are beautiful take deliberate and consistent time, attention, and work. From fertilizing to watering, mowing, weeding, and raking, lawns that are beautiful do not just happen. Neither do beautiful marriages. They require time, attention, and work.

Healthy bank accounts, on the other hand, are achieved by more deposits being invested than withdrawals being made. Thoughtful actions, kind words, and expressions of affection are some of the many types of deposits in the marriage bank. Thoughtless actions, harsh words, and a distance in the emotional attachment of marriage are dramatic withdrawals. Healthy bank accounts and healthy marriages have far more deposits than withdrawals.

Invest several moments reading through Genesis 24. Your pastor will share more from this chapter in your session. It is interesting to remember that in the Old Testament era, marriages were arranged by the groom's father. Knowing how important it was for his son to marry the right woman, Abraham makes his servant promise he will not take for his son Isaac a bride from the pagan women who lived nearby.

Most of us are very happy that we live in a different day and age. You may very well love your father; however, you are probably very pleased that the selection of your mate is not pre-arranged by your dad. As you read the account of the servant seeking the Lord's direction in obtaining a wife for Isaac, write down several key things that demonstrate the importance of marriage and seeking the Lord's will. _____

_____

_____

The servant greatly respected Abraham, Isaac, and Rebekah. He gave first priority to the marriage of his master's son. Nothing was more important to the servant than doing the will of his master. There are several very important principles to glean from this text. Each principle will relate to respect and priority, which are key elements in a healthy marriage relationship.

Work on this section during your counseling session

Your pastor will direct you to Genesis 24 and will share important principles with you. Notice the plan of the Lord for Isaac and Rebekah.

My Personal Notes from this Counseling Session

_____

_____

_____

_____

As you approach your wedding day and future marriage, it is very important to have a clear understanding of what makes a marriage healthy. As your session continues, your counselor will discuss biblical principles that are timeless and essential. After reviewing these verses and statements, a clear definition of marriage should be established in your mind. Jot down additional notes in the margin.

Several Biblical Principles

It is _____

"It is not good that the man should be alone; I will make him an help meet for him...Made he a woman, and brought her unto the man...Therefore shall a man leave his father and his mother, and shall cleave unto his wife: and they were both naked, the man and his wife, and were not ashamed" (Genesis 2:18-25).

Though many couples are choosing to ignore marriage, you are demonstrating by your premarital counseling that you believe in marriage. Congratulations! Marriage is important. It is God's idea.

It is _____

"Marriage is honorable in all, and the bed undefiled" (Hebrews 13:4a). The word for "honorable" is *timios* (TIM-ee-os) which means, "That which is

precious, of great price or held in high esteem." That which is honorable or precious within marriage is still forbidden outside of marriage (13:4b).

It is _____

"Have ye not read, that he which made them at the beginning made them male and female, and said, For this cause shall a man leave father and mother, and cleave to his wife: and they two shall be one flesh? Wherefore they are no more two, but one flesh" (Matthew 19:4-6a). The concept of "one flesh" is an intense connection of spiritual, emotional, physical, and sexual intimacy between one man and one woman within the gift of marriage.

It is _____

"What therefore God hath joined together, let not man put asunder" (Matthew 19:6b). It is important to understand that the decision you are making and the vows you will be taking are not a contract that has clauses and loopholes. This is a lasting covenant that is for "richer or poorer, for better or worse, in sickness and in health, as long as life shall last." Divorce is not an option. This aspect of the permanence of marriage must be emphasized and can never be overstated.

It is _____

"Wives, submit yourselves unto your own husbands, as unto the Lord. For the husband is the head of the wife, even as Christ is the head of the church: and he is the saviour of the body. Therefore as the church is subject unto Christ, so let the wives be to their own husbands in every thing. Husbands, love your wives, even as Christ also loved the church, and gave himself for it; that he might sanctify and cleanse it with the washing of water by the word, that he might present it to himself a glorious church, not having spot, or wrinkle, or any such thing; but that it should be holy and without blemish. So ought men to love their wives....For this cause shall a man leave his father and mother, and shall be joined unto his wife, and they two shall be one flesh. This is a great mystery: but I speak concerning Christ and the church. Nevertheless let every one of you in particular so love his wife even as himself; and the wife see that she reverence her husband" (Ephesians 5:22-33).

The role of the godly wife pictures the great reverence of the church for the Lord Jesus. Likewise, the devotion and love of the Lord Jesus directed toward His church is a wonderful model of the love and devotion of the godly husband. The illustration is powerful and practical.

It is _____

"Submitting yourselves one to another in the fear of God" (Ephesians 5:21). This is the opposite of the "me first" mentality so evident in the world today. There are many advocates of the view, "I am the most important person in the world," who selfishly demand happiness regardless of who is hurt and what the cost.

Mutual submission is the decision of the will to purposely view your mate as a higher priority than yourself. It is your willing service to seek the well-being of your mate rather than exalting yourself and demanding your personal rights. This does not mean that you neglect your personal well-being. Rather, you find great fulfillment in giving the Lord first priority, your mate the second priority, and yourself the third.

Respect and priority are two essential elements of a great marriage. Both must be evidenced now and growing at the time of the marriage. Without these two critical ingredients, your marriage will be in trouble before it begins.

Your counselor will share several very important ways respect and priority are demonstrated. He will review your answers to the assignment of Mark and Mindy.

Additional Notes from this Counseling Session

_____

_____

_____

_____

Your pastor-counselor greatly desires to help you prepare for your marriage. He can prepare you only to the extent that you are open and honest with him about your situation. If there are areas that you do not understand, ask him. If there are areas of respect and priority he has not covered, share your questions with him.

In the next section, you will be working on a significant homework assignment that will require a little more time than usual to complete. The assignment is entitled "The Road Already Traveled." Give yourself plenty of time to answer the questions and submit them to your pastor before your next appointment. If possible, make copies of your homework. This will allow you to keep your answers as part of your wedding keepsake.

Your response to these questions will be the basis for the next several premarital counseling sessions.

A Great Marriage— Settle for Nothing Less

Each premarital counseling session has a very specific purpose. The Lord desires that you would aim high! Do not settle for an average or mediocre marriage. Settle for nothing less than determining to have a great marriage.

Sadly, many marriages are failing today. The damage and heartbreak from such failure are devastating. Even in homes where the couples stay together, sometimes the marriage is not very happy. Marriages that are characterized by thoughtlessness, carelessness, and selfishness will never reach the level of joy and blessing that God intends.

Enter this counseling session with joy and anticipation. Your counselor will review and emphasize things you may already know. However, the time will be of great value because, once again, you will have the opportunity to apply the dynamic and precious principles God has for your marriage. Also during this session, you may be confronted with new principles and directives you have not considered before. It will be exciting to see what God has planned for you in this session.

Work on this section before your counseling session

Make arrangements with the pastor to make a copy of your test answers before your next counseling session.

While it is important to complete the entire test, it does not have to be done in one sitting. As you get started on this assignment, you will see that it will take a little time to complete. Answer each question thoughtfully, but do not take a long time analyzing each statement.

Sections 1 and 2 will be used as the basis for this premarital counseling session. Your counselor will need sufficient time to review your answers as well as the answers of your future mate. Do not discuss your answers with your future mate before the counseling session. On the basis of your answers, your counselor will design a unique counseling session for you. Your counselor may prefer to make copies of your answers. This would be preferable rather than tearing the pages from your book.

"The Road Already Traveled"

Homework for Premarital Counseling Sessions 3-5, and Postmarital Session.

Name _____

The information you are sharing will be held in strict confidence. Your counselor greatly desires to assist you in preparing for your marriage and home by helping you to understand your background. You have been traveling a road that has brought you to the point in life where the strong points can be strengthened and weak areas identified and changed before you enter marriage.

Please answer the questions in sections one through four by using the following scale of 1 to 4.

1= Very strongly disagree, as this almost never describes my situation.
2= Mildly disagree, as this usually does not describe my situation.
3= Mildly agree, as this sometimes describes my situation.
4= Strongly agree, as this usually describes my situation.

1. How I view marriage as modeled before me

_____ 1. I had the privilege of a close relationship with at least one set of grandparents.

_____ 2. I had the privilege of knowing my grandparents were happily married.

_____ 3. My grandparents were role models of how a happy marriage works.

_____ 4. I would describe my parents as happily married.

_____ 5. My parents openly express their love for each other.

_____ 6. I have frequently witnessed my parents being affectionate with other.

_____ 7. My parents love the Lord and our home. Though not perfect, it is a model of what I would like my home to be.

_____ 8. I know the role of being a spiritual leader because it was consistently modeled in our home.

_____ 9. Family time in reading the Bible and praying was common in my home.

_____ 10. I remember great family times spent together as well as special times on vacation.

2. How I view my relationship with the Lord

_____ 1. I know the Lord as my personal Savior and seek to live for Him.

_____ 2. I want to know and do the will of God because it provides great priorities in my life.

_____ 3. I read the Bible on a nearly daily basis.

_____ 4. I am a member of a Bible-believing church.

_____ 5. I have a regular ministry in my church.

_____ 6. I can honestly say my future mate and I agree on the importance of living for Christ and both of us are seeking to live for Him.

_____ 7. I have witnessed my future mate reading the Bible, praying and serving in some area of Christian service in our local church.

_____ 8. I am encouraged that my future mate is consistent in praying with me on a regular basis.

_____ 9. I can honestly say my future mate and I talk regularly about spiritual matters.

_____ 10. I know my future mate is growing spiritually and is becoming a mature disciple of the Lord Jesus Christ.

3. How I view things relating to my future home and marriage

_____ 1. My future mate and I have a strong relationship of trust and mutual respect.

_____ 2. My future mate and I have talked about finances, and budgeting, and are in agreement with how our finances will be handled.

_____ 3. My future mate and I have talked about the things that make a marriage strong.

_____ 4. My future mate has a good relationship with his or her parents.

_____ 5. I have a good relationship with my parents.

_____ 6. My future mate and I have talked about the relationship we wish to have with both sets of parents after we are married.

_____ 7. My future mate and I agree on tithing and regular giving to the local church.

_____ 8. My future mate and I have talked about parenting and how to raise children.

_____ 9. My future mate and I are in agreement with the number of children we would like to have.

_____ 10. My future mate and I are in agreement with how we would like to spend holidays and vacation.

4. My current situation

_____ 1. Financially, I live within my means and adhere to a budget.

_____ 2. Financially, my mate lives within his/her means and adheres to a budget.

_____ 3. My future mate and I have a good level of communication and I am satisfied with it.

_____ 4. I feel like I can talk with my future mate about anything and will have his/her attention and understanding.

_____ 5. My future mate and I are currently serving the Lord in some capacity.

5. My walk with the Lord

(In this section, simply check the statements that best describe you.)

_____ I know the Lord as Savior

_____ I sometimes doubt my salvation

_____ I struggle with the assurance of salvation

_____ I am growing in my spiritual life

_____ I read the Bible nearly daily

_____ I pray throughout the day

_____ I am assured my future mate knows the Lord as personal Savior

_____ I grew up in a Christian home

_____ I am the first Christian in my family

_____ My future mate and I pray regularly together

_____ My future mate and I agree on the church in which we will be members

_____ My mate and I agree on how frequently we will attend our local church

_____ My mate and I enjoying serving in our local church

_____ The Lord has first priority in my life

6. Which of the following statements best describe you?

_____ Outgoing, friendly

_____ Enjoys meeting people

_____ Enthusiastic

_____ Undisciplined

_____ Exaggerates at times

_____ Cold, unsympathetic

_____ Unforgiving

_____ Opinionated

_____ Productive

_____ Self confident

_____ Easy going

_____ Dependable

_____ Unmotivated

_____ Indecisive

_____ Analytical

_____ Sensitive

_____ Moody

_____ Revengeful

_____ Humorous, funny

_____ Talkative

_____ Generous

_____ Disorganized

_____ Can be insensitive

_____ Hostile, angry

_____ Domineering

_____ Proud

_____ Practical, logical

_____ Calm, quiet

_____ Diplomatic

_____ Reluctant leader

_____ Stubborn

_____ Fearful

_____ Perfectionist

_____ Self sacrificing

_____ Critical

_____ Very loving

7. Which of the following statements best describe your future mate?

_____ Outgoing, friendly	_____ Humorous, funny
_____ Enjoys meeting people	_____ Talkative
_____ Enthusiastic	_____ Generous
_____ Undisciplined	_____ Disorganized
_____ Exaggerates at times	_____ Can be insensitive
_____ Cold, unsympathetic	_____ Hostile, angry
_____ Unforgiving	_____ Domineering
_____ Opinionated	_____ Proud
_____ Productive	_____ Practical, logical
_____ Self confident	_____ Calm, quiet
_____ Easy going	_____ Diplomatic
_____ Dependable	_____ Reluctant leader
_____ Unmotivated	_____ Stubborn
_____ Indecisive	_____ Fearful
_____ Analytical	_____ Perfectionist
_____ Sensitive	_____ Self sacrificing
_____ Moody	_____ Critical
_____ Revengeful	_____ Very loving

8. **Select the following statements that best describe the home in which you grew up.**

_____	I was an only child	_____	Godly father
_____	Godly mother	_____	Spiritually-minded home
_____	Warm, loving	_____	Love was demonstrated
_____	Fun, laughter	_____	Generally happy home
_____	People visited often	_____	Devotions together
_____	Cold, unloving	_____	Harsh, demanding
_____	Perfectionist demands	_____	Spontaneous
_____	Quiet, lonely at times	_____	Often noisy, activities
_____	Organized, orderly	_____	Well disciplined
_____	Too permissive	_____	Too disciplined
_____	Favoritism shown	_____	Good parenting
_____	Regular vacations	_____	All shared chores
_____	Talked together	_____	Ignored problems
_____	Resolved problems	_____	Generous

_____ Often had at least one meal together daily

_____ Respect shown   _____ Respect taught consistently

9. **Select the following statements that best describe the home in which your future partner grew up.**

_____	I was an only child	_____	Godly father
_____	Godly mother	_____	Spiritually minded home
_____	Warm, loving	_____	Love was demonstrated

_____ Fun, laugher   _____ Generally happy home

_____ People visited often   _____ Devotions together

_____ Cold, unloving   _____ Harsh, demanding

_____ Perfectionist demands   _____ Spontaneous

_____ Quiet, lonely at times   _____ Often noisy, activities

_____ Organized, orderly   _____ Well disciplined

_____ Too permissive   _____ Too disciplined

_____ Favoritism shown   _____ Good parenting

_____ Regular vacations   _____ All shared chores

_____ Talked together   _____ Ignored problems

_____ Resolved problems   _____ Generous

_____ Often had at least one meal together daily

_____ Respect shown   _____ Respect taught consistently

10. Complete the following statements in your own words.

A. When I think about marriage, I feel-_____

_____

B. Some of the things I appreciate about my future mate include-_____

_____

_____

C. Among my expectations in marriage, several that are very important to me include-_____

_____

D. Several areas that need to improve in my life would include- _____

_____

Several areas that need to improve in the life of my future mate would include-_____

_____

E. When I think of the number of children I would like to have it would be-

_____

F. When I think of the ideal way of spending an evening together with my future mate, it would be-_____

_____

G. When I think of the ideal vacation, it would be-_____

_____

Work on this section during your counseling session

This is one of the most special times in your life. You and your future mate have a great opportunity to commit to making your marriage truly great. The acrostic G-R-E-A-T will bring into focus the essential elements of a "great" marriage.

G= Godliness that is consistent in daily living
R= Realistic expectations of myself and my mate
E= Endurance and endearment, as divorce is never an option
A= Affirmation and affection are genuinely extended
T= Truthfulness, tactfulness, and tenderness are expressed consistently and daily

There are no perfect marriages. However, your marriage can be great! Settling for mediocrity in surgery, construction, accounting, and marriage are not wise choices. As you prepare for your marriage, it will be an interesting time of honestly evaluating your picture of marriage and what has been modeled before you.

Do you have the privilege of being part of a multi-generational family who loves the Lord and enjoys great marriages? Or, on the other hand, do you have the great opportunity of being the first generation in your family to begin a new line of godliness and great marriages?

It may sound very strange to you to think of grandchildren. However, have you recently read Deuteronomy 6:1-2? Moses instructed the second-generation children of Israel to build a strong home and family for the sake of their children and grandchildren. In a very real sense, everything you are currently deciding and implementing is paving the way for your future children and grandchildren.

What would you like to leave as an inheritance for your grandchildren? Take a moment to read Proverbs 13:22 and consider wisely the application. In the years ahead, your grandchildren should be able to say the following of you as their grandparent:

1. Concerning Christ, my grandparent trusted Him fully (Acts 16:31).

2. Concerning the Bible, my grandparent treasured it dearly (Psalm 119:72, 127).

3. Concerning sin, my grandparent turned from it deliberately (Romans 6:22).

4. Concerning blessings, my grandparent thanked the Lord joyfully (Psalms 95, 100).

5. Concerning the children and grandchildren, my grandparent taught us diligently (Deuteronomy 6:7).

You will work through several issues with your counselor concerning your spiritual walk with the Lord, the home in which you grew up, and the marriage modeled before you in your parent's home.

Take good notes with the Scripture references shared during your counseling session. Do not hesitate to ask questions and be very open and honest with your counselor.

Without being critical of your home and parents, think carefully and honestly concerning how marriage has been modeled before you. Was love expressed consistently, and if so, how? Did you come from a godly background? What kind of spiritual leadership did you consistently see? Currently, are you and your future mate walking with the Lord?

In Deuteronomy chapter 6, the children of Israel were instructed to build a strong marriage, home, and family. This would be demonstrated in their current generation as well as in the lives of their children and grandchildren. Wise couples make the same spiritual goals as did the children of Israel.

My Personal Notes from this Counseling Session

_____

_____

_____

_____

Your pastor will ask you to work on the financial planner found in the next chapter and the following questions before your next appointment.

Work on these questions after your counseling session

During the next several weeks, you and your future mate will discover much about each other as you quietly, gently and honestly answer the questions from "Let's Share—Great Questions and Honest Answers." This is not time wasted. Rather, your answers to these questions will be a great investment in preparing you for a strong and growing marriage. While not perfect, your marriage truly can be a great blessing and deeply rewarding.

Listed are fifty questions to discuss with your future mate. Do not try to answer every question in one sitting. Make a high priority in selecting a good time to honestly share with each other and discover things about yourself and your future partner. Make this a wonderful time of prayer, Bible study, and discovery. If you encounter a question in which you and your future mate struggle to answer, simply write it down and bring it with you to your next premarital counseling session.

May the Lord bring you great joy and growth as you work through these questions.

"Let's Share-Great Questions and Honest Answers"

1. How do you see our careers impacting our marriage in both good and possibly difficult ways?
2. What are our individual goals relating to our careers?
3. How long do we want to wait before trying to have a baby?
4. How many children would we hope to have someday?
5. What if one of us is ready to begin our family and the other is not? How will we resolve this?
6. What will some of the changes be in our home and personal lives when the Lord allows us to have a child?
7. Are we agreed as to the method of birth control we want to use? Have we worked through this sufficiently in our minds after receiving good counsel from our physician and pastor? Are we sure this method prevents pregnancy and does not terminate it?
8. What are our plans as relating to housing? Which will work best for us right now: renting or purchasing a home?
9. How large a place do we think we really need right now?
10. How much of our income should we spend on housing? If we are not sure, are we willing to discuss this with our pastor in the premarital counseling time?
11. How important is money in our relationship?
12. What are three or four material possessions we would like to acquire someday that will require savings and a significant investment?
13. How do we define financial security?
14. What should be our attitude about indebtedness?
15. How many credit cards should we have?
16. How important should it be to pay off the balance on our credit card or cards every month?
17. Should we have a joint checking account or should we have separate accounts?

18. How much should we save each month and how we will invest our saving?
19. Even though retirement is a long way off, how much should we invest in our retirement account? How much should we tuck away in an emergency fund?
20. What are some of the things we will enjoy doing together around the house?
21. Will we grocery shop together? If not, whose responsibility should this be?
22. Who will be responsible for cooking? Will we share this responsibility together, and if so, how?
23. What about household chores? How will we share in these?
24. How often would we enjoy eating out?
25. How important is dating after we are married?
26. How often will we go out with our friends?
27. How often will we entertain friends in our home?
28. What are some of the good things we appreciate in the home and marriage of our parents which we would like to bring into our home and marriage?
29. What are some things we would like to change and incorporate into our home and marriage?
30. What are some of the possible conflicts that might arise out of our personality differences? How will we deal with these possibilities?
31. How will we handle holidays with our families?
32. How we will handle vacations?
33. How will we work through conflicts without hurting each other?
34. What place will the Lord hold in our home and marriage?
35. How important is daily worship and prayer as individuals and as a couple?
36. What will be our local church?
37. How important will it be in our marriage for us to serve the Lord?
38. If someday a missions trip should become a possibility, would we be willing to prayerfully consider going together?
39. What does a healthy marriage look like to us?
40. What does the role of a good husband look like? What does the role of a good wife look like?
41. What do we think a healthy sexual relationship would seem to be?

42. How often do we hope to have sex in a typical week?
43. How will we handle it when one is interested in having sex and the other is not?
44. How much do we honestly understand about the difference between a man's view of sex and a woman's view of sex?
45. How will we make big decisions together?
46. What if we discover someday that we cannot have children? Would we ever be willing to consider adoption?
47. What do we appreciate about me? What are some areas that I really need to be working on?
48. Why do you want to marry me?
49. Would we be willing to speak with our pastor and go for marriage counseling if someday we encounter a situation we cannot resolve ourselves?
50. What are several major safeguards we want to establish to make sure our marriage stays healthy and grows throughout our lifetime?

Write out any additional questions you desire to discuss.

_____

_____

_____

_____

_____

List any question or topic you wish to have addressed in your next counseling session. Be sure to alert your counselor ahead of time.

_____

_____

_____

_____

_____

My View of Home and Marriage

The first several months of your marriage will be marked by two very wonderful words. These are *discovery* and *adjustment*. As your wedding approaches, you are beginning to discover more and more about your beloved sweetheart. In this counseling session, your pastor-counselor will be using your answers from testing areas 3 and 4 in "The Road Already Traveled" as well as your estimates on "Our Financial Planner."

Work on this section before your counseling session

Your pastor will be interested to find out how you are doing with the questions from the previous section. How many things have you discovered about yourself? What have you learned about your future partner? What are two or three things you are praying about and working on with the Lord right now? _____

_____

Reaching Agreement on Important Issues

The unity of your marriage and home will be greatly enhanced if you come to agreement about several key things. Wise couples seek to reach agreement on trust, mutual respect, budgeting, finances, their relationship with parents, and plans for future children. These topics are covered in this counseling session.

Mutual trust experienced and extended in your relationship

How would you define the word *trust*? Among the many definitions you might list, trust is the sense of security and confidence one has in the life of his or her future mate. While understanding that your sweetheart is not perfect, it will be important to establish a relationship of mutual trust. What are several things you must do to help your future mate trust in you?

_____

_____

_____

_____

Financial considerations to establish in our home and marriage

One of the great dangers facing every marriage is out-of-control financial indebtedness and disaster. This danger is marked by several warning signs:

1. There are patterns of wasteful spending that are depleting the funds of the couple. Many times, the money is wasted by spending it a little here and a little there with little to show for it.

2. Impulsive buying and spending sprees by one or both of the bridal couple. An impulsive buyer looks only at the here and now. Impulsive purchases are made on items that often are not needed or used, and sometimes, are not even desirable.

3. Out-of-control credit card use and indebtedness. Society makes it very easy for couples to satisfy themselves quickly with little effort. Then comes the bill next month, and funds are not available to pay off the card. Additional debt is added by making minimum payments. Before the couple knows it, the credit card company becomes a master, and they are slaves to repaying it.

You as a couple will need to work on this financial planner. While this form is not exhaustive in budgeting possibilities, it will give you a good idea of what to expect and how to plan for wise financial living. You may need to project what you anticipate your expenses to be, but do your best to be realistic.

Our Financial Planner

Monthly Income

Gross Monthly Income   _____

Investment Income   _____

Total Monthly Income   _____

Monthly Deductions

Tithe and Offering   _____

Federal Income Tax   _____

State/Local Taxes   _____

Social Security/Medicare   _____

Total Monthly Gross Income   _____

Total Monthly Tithe/ Taxes   _____

Total Remaining Usable Monthly Income _____

Expenses: Housing Payments

Mortgage/Rent   _____

Homeowners/ Renters Ins.   _____

Property Taxes   _____

Repairs/Improvements   _____

Utilities:

Electric _____   Gas _____

Water/Sewer _____   Telephone _____

Total Housing Expenses _____

Expenses: Food and Grocery _____

Expenses: Heath Ins. Medical Exp. _____

Expenses: Transportation

Car Payment _____

Insurance _____

Gas/Oil/Repairs _____

Misc. Tolls/Parking _____

Total Transportation _____

Expenses: Credit Card/Loans _____

**Expenses: Entertainment/
Recreation/Personal** _____

Savings/ Investments _____

Total Monthly Usable Income _____

Total Monthly Projected Expenses _____

Current Status (Positive or Negative) _____

Mature couples are timely in paying their bills and assuming responsibility for their finances. Do you and your future mate have a godly view of stewardship? Do you honor the Lord in your finances (Proverbs 3:9-10)? Certainly the Lord is glorified (1 Corinthians 10:31) by maintaining a good credit score with timely payments and financial integrity. This is a wonderful opportunity for you as a couple to develop godly convictions in the area of your tithe, offerings, and generosity with the Lord.

As a couple, it will be very important to invest time together in prayer as well as preparation for this session. Working together on your financial planner will be helpful before you arrive for your counseling session.

Good communication with my future mate

You will not only talk about your relationship with the Lord and your handling of finances in this session, but you will also have the opportunity of thinking through your present level of communication. It is not uncommon for the man to be satisfied with the present level of communication, while the lady is very dissatisfied. Many men are startled when their future mate scores a low number on the level of satisfaction for communication.

It will be important for you to begin to establish good communication skills now in your relationship. Are your parents good role models in communication? How does the future bride speak to her father? How does the future groom speak to his mother? These often provide glimpses into the future level of respect communicated in marriage.

Words can easily become deadly bullets fired carelessly toward the marriage partner. These word bullets are tones of sarcasm, ridicule, needless accusations, negatively comparing the marriage partner with others, hurtful put downs, negative facial gesturing and hateful words. James was right: the use of the tongue and our words can cause great damage (James 3:1-10).

The opposite of the damaging tongue is also true. Relationships, friendships, and marriages are greatly encouraged and nurtured by the appropriate use of godly words. King David said, *"I will take heed to my ways, that I sin not with my tongue"* (Psalm 39:1). The writer of Proverbs declared, *"The wholesome tongue is a tree of life"* (Proverbs 15:4). Wise couples learn early the importance of good communication. Listen with an open mind. Look at your partner when he or she is speaking. Refrain from interrupting. Think about what your partner has said. Even if one disagrees, respect and thoughtfulness must be shown.

Your counselor will share with you his observations of your communication during the counseling process. Ephesians 4:15 reminds us to be *"Speaking the truth in love."* This will ensure that maturing can take place. It may not be easy to confront weak areas of communication. However, it is much better to address these areas now rather than later in your marriage.

Work on this section during your counseling session

Take detailed notes from this session as your counselor shares several principles upon which strong marriages are built. Think of the acrostic "WAFFLE" in the building of strong and beautiful marriages. The principles may sound simple; but the consistent application will result in great blessing.

Additionally, your pastor will work through your answers from sections 3 and 4 of "The Road Already Traveled" and the financial planner as well.

My Personal Notes from this Counseling Session

_____

_____

_____

_____

Your pastor will ask you to read and answer the questions to "The Journey of Ron and Lisa." This will help you to prepare for counseling session 5. Additional homework may be assigned by your pastor based on situations addressed in your counseling session today.

Making a Marriage That Works and Grows

As a couple, you are continuing to work through specific areas in preparing for your life together as husband and wife. These days are no doubt ones in which you find yourself growing in excitement, but also sensing the great responsibility of being a married partner.

Every couple enjoys a host of common things shared with each other. Several things that you share in common with other couples include:

1. Every couple has a background from which they travel.

2. Every couple has a set of preferences, opinions, and values or convictions that have been taught (by direct instruction) as well as caught (by observation).

3. Every couple has sinful human natures that at times are manifested in very unpleasant ways.

4. Every couple brings two distinct personalities into the marriage that may complement each other or clash with each other.

5. Every couple has the potential of becoming the married partners the Lord intends. What a wonderful working and growing marriage God desires for you!

Work on this section before your counseling session

The choices before you are enormous. This is a critical time of decision-making as to the direction your marriage, home, and family will take. Choose to side with Joshua when he declared, *"And if it seem evil unto you to serve the LORD, choose you this day whom ye will serve...but as for me and my house, we will serve the LORD*" (Joshua 24:15). There is no better time to commit to the Lord to become a "Joshua" kind of marriage and household.

Your counselor will be exploring the answers you gave in sections 5-9 of "The Road Already Traveled." Also, complete the answers to the following homework and submit them to the pastor at least two weeks before your next appointment.

The Journey of Ron and Lisa

Homework for Premarital Counseling Session 5

"Getting to Know the Real Me"

> Ron and Lisa have been married for thirteen years. Though they grew up in the same general area in the rural farming lands of Iowa, their backgrounds are very different. As you read the story of their marriage journey, think through the importance of understanding your mate as well as yourself.
>
> Ron's family were hard-working farmers who seldom took time off as they worked from before dawn until late in the day, almost everyday. Ron's mom and dad were young children when their individual families both moved to Iowa to work the land. Five brothers and three sisters caused Ron's life to be filled with noise, laughter, and times of rivalry that caused mom to swat the children with a rolled up towel! "Out of my kitchen and stop that racket!" often were the words mom shouted in good nature and with a smile as she scooted the children on their way.
>
> The Lord was the center of the life of Ron's family. Though the farm required many hours every day, the Lord was honored early in the morning. Individually each member of the family had quiet moments in the Word of God and prayer. Breakfast took place together after dad had already worked several hours. No food was served until dad carefully took the old family Bible off the shelf in the kitchen and brought it to the table. The atmosphere was not harsh or rigid. How-

ever, each child knew this was not the time to wiggle or giggle. Dad read a portion of the Word and one of the children would be asked to lead in prayer and thank the Lord for the day and the food. As soon as the "Amen" was spoken, all quietness and serenity were shattered as massive amounts of food were passed and most of the family talked at the same time.

Immediately after supper, as soon as the dishes were taken to the sink, the family gathered in the living room of the old farm house for what was called "evening worship." Ron's mom often played a hymn or two on the old upright piano. Even though it was not in tune and even though the family was not composed of great singers, wonderful times of music and worship took place around that old piano. Dad would often read from the Bible and then make up a story of his own that would illustrate what the family read.

The children grew older and one by one left the home for college or marriage. The family circle grew smaller. Ron, who was number six in the line of nine children, was old enough to remember the great evenings of large family gatherings in that small living room. Even better were the times when guests were present and everything stopped for "evening worship." By the time Ron was preparing for marriage, the family gatherings were less than half the size; but precious still in the learning of God's ways and growing as a family of believers.

Ron had a personality that was very outgoing. He loved to meet people and conversation came easily for him. As Ron would be sent into town on an errand, dad would often remind him, "Ronnie, get back here with the tractor part as soon as you can. Don't stop and talk with everyone you meet." Ron would laugh and wave to his dad as he jumped into his rusty pickup that had over 314,000 miles on it. Dust from the driveway flew as Ron headed to town eagerly waiting who he might see at the parts supply store.

Everyone seemed to love Ron's sense of humor and generosity. He was funny, but he still had a concern for others that was demonstrated by his impulsive willingness to share. Sometimes Ron gave away most of his paycheck because someone else had a need. Later, there would be a time or two when he would have trouble paying a bill because with little or no thought of his own needs; he gave away a large part of his paycheck.

Enthusiasm was second nature to Ron. Nothing daunted him. He awoke long before the alarm would go off. Eager and excited about the day, Ron often annoyed the two other brothers who shared the room but did not share the same outlook. By the time the alarm would sound, Ron had already thought of two jokes, ten questions and fifteen things to talk about. The other two brothers were simply trying to remember where they were and what day it was! Pillows often flew at Ron as the other brothers covered their heads with their blankets.

Ron had a hard time understanding why others were not as cheerful and excited about life. Lisa had noticed Ron on several occasions. He was always talking with someone and frequently would end the conversation with laughter and a gentle slap on the shoulder of the other men as he left the group. She would not be noticed by Ron until Lisa's family visited the church where Ron and his family attended. Right in the middle of the hymn Ron glanced in Lisa's direction and spotted her. There, right before his eyes, was the most beautiful young woman he had ever seen. Ron didn't get very much out of the service that Sunday. Though Ron had often been accused of exaggerating, this time Ron really meant it when he whispered to himself, "She is the most incredibly beautiful woman I have ever seen." The service could not end fast enough for Ron that Sunday. Several were surprised that Ron didn't speak in return to them as he flew past six pews of worshippers to meet the beautiful, but very shy and introverted, Lisa.

She spotted him coming. It would be no exaggeration to say she could feel her face starting to burn as she knew it was turning red. Oh, to stop that blushing. "Why does it always come at the worst time in the world?" she thought. Ron introduced himself and began to talk non-stop. His normal extroverted personality seemed in overdrive as he talked with the visitor named Lisa.

Lisa's family lived in the neighboring town about twenty miles from Ron and his family. Hard work was a normal part of their lives but farming was not the family business. Lisa's dad was a professor in a local community college, and her mother taught in the elementary school in town. Lisa was the oldest of the sibling group of three daughters. She and her family were close and enjoyed doing things together.

Lisa's personality was very quiet, calm and easygoing. Often she heard her parents talk about the need to find a church somewhere, sometime. She never pressed the issue, assuming that sooner or later they would get around to it. Studies came fairly easy to Lisa. That was a huge blessing, because Lisa often would procrastinate in many areas, including her school work. Even though mom and dad were in public education, Lisa had the attitude of "When it comes to term papers, why start today what could be put off until tomorrow?"

There were times of tension in the family between her parents and Lisa as mom and dad did not share this same viewpoint. Though she was a procrastinator, Lisa was very dependable. She was never early on completing an assignment, but she was consistently on time. She was totally dependable in other areas as well. Seldom did Lisa miss an obligation or fail to keep a promise.

Without a doubt, the most difficult thing in the world for Lisa was to make decisions. One of the reasons she would procrastinate on her term papers was found in trying to decide the subject for her writing. This difficulty in making decisions translated into most areas of her life. Many times her sisters would become impatient with her as they waited for her to decide which sweater to wear or what color slacks to select. Several times she was left behind because she was having trouble making up her mind again.

Lisa's family had very little interest in spiritual things. That started to change when a good friend died suddenly as the result of a tragic automobile accident. Lisa's family was deeply moved at the funeral service conducted by Pastor Winters. They were impressed by his gentle and loving remarks. His message directly from the Bible was amazing and something brand new to them. However, it was the loving and caring congregation of the church who reached out to the family of the deceased friend that convinced Lisa's family that something big was missing in their lives. Whatever this congregation had, Lisa's family needed.

Two weeks later, during an appointment Lisa's dad had made with Pastor Winters, Lisa's family together placed their faith in Christ. Pastor Winters could not remember the last time he led an entire family to the Lord. Lisa's family would visit Pastor Winters church the next Sunday.

True to form, while everyone else was very nervous about this new activity for Sunday morning, Lisa was even-keeled and collected. The hardest part of the entire morning for her was to decide between her yellow dress and the pink outfit which was given to her for her last birthday. The rest of the family was heading for the car when she finally decided on the yellow outfit. Dad had to drive hurriedly to keep from being late. Lisa noticed Ron that first Sunday but was too shy to hardly look up when he and a group of friends walked near by.

It was on the second visit that Ron had discovered her. Soon they began dating and truly enjoyed getting to know each other. Lisa found Ron amusing, funny, and animated, never running out of good stories or sharing news of things that were going on in his life. Lisa was so easy to date. She seldom had a preference as to where they would eat a bite of lunch together. Ron did notice that she seemed to have a hard time deciding even on little things on the menu. She was a good and calming influence in his life, and he encouraged her to be a little more outgoing. A year later they were engaged, and six months later they married.

Now thirteen years and two children ages 9 and 6 later, Ron and Lisa are making an appointment for marriage counseling. Pastor Winters has retired, but their current Pastor has scheduled an intake session to gather information and data about Ron and Lisa.

Ron has told the pastor, "I love my wife, but she never gets around to anything. She has unfinished projects all over the house. I don't think she even loves me anymore. She never is affectionate. She is unresponsive to me in every way. And stubborn- I want to tell you pastor, is she ever stubborn!"

Through her tears, Lisa said, "Pastor, I can see why my husband feels this way. But he has pushed me away. He makes promises he does not keep. He has forgotten both my birthday and our anniversary. He talks; but never stops to listen. In fact, he is always talking, talking,

talking; but never listening. We are behind in our bills because Ron has insisted on helping his sister and her family. I am sorry they are out of work; but we have bills too. When I tried to tell him how concerned about this I was, he made a joke about it and gave them additional funds. I really don't think my husband loves us. He is always running here and there to help everyone else."

Imagine you are the counseling pastor.

1. What are several key characteristics of Ron's personality? _____

   _____

2. What are several key characteristics of Lisa's personality? _____

   _____

3. What are several key areas in which the two different personalities complement each other? _____

   _____

4. What are several key areas in which the two different personalities clash? _____

   _____

5. What are several key characteristics of your personality? _____

   _____

6. What are several key characteristics of your future mate's personality?

   _____

   _____

7. What are several ways your personalities complement each other?

   _____

   What are several ways your personalities clash? _____

   _____

Your counselor has invested time and prayer in designing a session unique to you as a couple. It is a tremendous blessing to know that you are not only special to the Lord, but you are special to your pastor-counselor as well. He has carefully reviewed your tests and compared your answers for complementing areas and potential areas that may conflict.

Work on this section during your counseling session

You may have already discovered areas of strengths and weaknesses, not only in yourself, but in your sweetheart. King David wrote, "*Search me, O God, and know my heart: try me, and know my thoughts: and see if there be any wicked way in me, and lead me in the way everlasting*" (Psalm 139:23-24).

This is an important time to ask the Lord not only to search you, but to help you to be honest with Him, yourself, your future mate, and your counselor. You may find this session somewhat uncomfortable at times. However, it is much wiser to address these situations now and resolve them before your wedding, rather than to have them surfacing as major problems after the wedding. Your pastor will share key principles to accept and remember.

Key Principles to Accept and Remember

My Personal Notes from this Counseling Session

_____

_____

_____

_____

Your counselor has shared several areas in your backgrounds as well as personalities that complement each other. He has no doubt invested more time sharing areas he sees as potential conflicts. Do not be discouraged. Be honest. Be committed to addressing and resolving them.

In Paul's writing to the Ephesian believers, he sets forth several dynamic scriptural principles for resolving conflicts. Pretending that the conflict is not there will not help. Getting even with your future mate for the conflict also will not help. Clamming up and giving your future mate the silent, cold-war treatment not only doesn't help; it makes matters worse. While not a simple, quick-fix remedy, Ephesians 4 will provide the long-term formula for dealing with most conflicts, including those in marriage.

Biblically resolving conflicts

1. Always attack the problem; never attack each other (4:15).

2. Identify the situation and call it what it really is—sin (4:22). Do not blame this on your parents. Do not blame others for this problem. Be willing to identify the works of the old sinful nature and acknowledge that they are sinful. Take the responsibility for your wrong actions and poor choices.

3. Ask the Lord to help you view the situation from a biblical perspective (4:23-24).

4. Be totally honest about your role in this matter (4:25). Do not be deceptive. Honesty along with loving graciousness and gentleness are important characteristics in establishing and maintaining a marriage that is fresh, growing, and vibrant.

5. Do not become defensive and "clam up," refusing to talk or speak about the conflict (4:26).

6. Ask the Lord to give you grace, not to become angry and explosive by saying things you will later regret (4:27).

7. Be willing to ask the Lord to make big changes in your personal life (4:28-32).

Total honesty and openness with your future mate involves willingness to admit there are areas in which you must improve. Do not be surprised if it is easier to see potentially weak or sinful areas in the life of your future mate than it is to recognize these areas in your own personal life. You need to trust your future partner to be willing to be honest with you and committed to working through the situations of your life. Talk with your future mate quietly, openly, graciously, and genuinely. Invest time together in prayer and Bible study. Heed carefully the pastor's counsel and observations.

Work on this section after your counseling session

Understanding the choices we make

Maturity is all about choices. Choose to address areas that require attention. Think of these concluding questions:

1. What are two or three significant issues through which your future mate and you must work? _____

   _____

2. What are several major areas in which you and your future mate have come to mutual understanding and resolution? _____

   _____

3. What about your spiritual condition? What are the similarities as well as differences in your spiritual convictions regarding your walk with the Lord? _____

   _____

4. How are you doing on the fifty questions? Are there any areas in which you have not yet reached an agreement? _____

   _____

5. Are there areas of concern that your pastor has not yet addressed? Be sure to bring these to his attention. _____

   _____

Think of one or two ways to express how much your sweetheart means to you this week. Do not allow your relationship to become stale. Next to the Lord, your future mate must become the most important person in the whole wide world to you.

As your wedding day draws near, here are three great challenges:

- Grow in your walk with the Lord.
- Be creative in your appreciation for your future partner.
- Look forward to your next counseling appointment!

The Goal and Joy of Intimacy

What is the first thought that comes into your mind when you hear the word *intimacy?* Some immediately think of the word *sex.* Did you? Actually, there is a significant difference between the experiences of intimacy and sexual intercourse. Understanding the importance of each is very important in avoiding marital failure and enjoying marital success.

Intimacy is the closeness of emotional bonding that is established between the husband and wife. This intimacy is not an automatic thing that somehow just happens all on its own. It must be nurtured, demonstrated, carefully guarded, and earnestly protected from those things that seek to destroy it.

Sexual activity is one expression of intimacy. This is the wonderful enjoyment of God's amazing gift given to couples within the safeguard and sanctity of marriage. No other human relationship comes close to matching the precious experience of *"Marriage is honorable in all, and the bed undefiled"* (Hebrews 13:4). Between the husband and wife, the abandonment of concealment, and the total desire to thrill, love, and express exhilarating physical, emotional, and sexual oneness is incredible.

Work on this section before your counseling session

Your pastor-counselor may surprise you when he uses himself and his qualification for ministry as an illustration. One of the qualifications for ministry is found in 1 Timothy 3:2, *"A bishop then must be blameless, the husband of one wife."* What do you think this means? _____

_____

_____

How does this relate to you and your marriage? _____

_____

Take the challenge. Accept nothing less. Set as your goal the joy and blessing of honest and consistent intimacy.

Understanding what intimacy is and how it is achieved

The primary picture of intimacy is that of bonding and closeness. It is often referred to by the word *connection*. The word *intimacy* is both beautiful and intense. The connection or intimacy between the husband and wife is that of being familiar, personal, or private with the love of your life. A commitment is made and consistently reinforced that your connection is of great value and that which is to be cherished. Thus, it must not be violated nor shared.

Biblical intimacy holds back nothing that is helpful or blessed from your marriage partner. It makes you vulnerable in that you give yourself totally to your mate. You are unclothed physically, emotionally, and personally with one who is not only your partner, but actually the extension of your own life. As a godly marriage partner, seek to live graciously, honestly, and openly with your mate. Additionally, seek to be creative to discover new and practical ways to communicate to your mate, "Next to the Lord, you are the most important person in the world." Therefore, you desire to share with your future mate the totality of your life, your body, your dreams, your desires, and your love.

Intimacy is always the goal for marriage. Some mistakenly associate the sexual act of marriage as being the only requirement for intimacy. This wonderful gift from God is actually only a part of the closeness of intimacy. There are times when a medical condition may make sexual activity impossible. Intimacy is still achievable for that couple.

Intimacy is the closeness and connection couples can experience even when sexual activity cannot take place. It is built upon trust, security, communication, and affection. This intimacy is fresh, growing, and of great value. Often, it is manifested with the statement, "My mate is not only my lover; he or she is also my very best friend."

The biblical picture of intimacy takes us back to the Garden of Eden and the experience of Adam with his wife. It will be time well worth the investment to think through this very familiar passage.

What was it like for Adam?

During your counseling session, your pastor will review these principles with you. Now is a good time to prepare for this session by carefully reading and considering the following biblical truths.

Adam's Placement (Genesis 2:8)

We can only imagine how wonderful the conditions were for Adam. The Lord planted a garden, and there He put the man. A "planted garden" and a "put man" by the LORD God describe the amazing surroundings. It will be important for you as a couple to be assured that only Adam's home was planted in such amazingly ideal surroundings; your home will be planted in the midst of surroundings that are far less than ideal. Therefore, it will be wise to seek the Lord's direction and blessing in all of your plans.

Adam's Assignment (Genesis 2:15)

Adam had two very important things to do in the Garden. First, he was to dress it. This gives the ideas of laboring or serving. He was to be busy serving in the role of God's worker in an ideal garden. Second, he was to keep it. This gives the idea of watching and waiting as well as being in charge. Adam was to serve and supervise in a beautiful and blessed place.

Adam's Aloneness and Apartness (Genesis 2:18-20)

An amazing situation was taking place in the ideal garden. Surrounded by beautiful flowers, plants, and rivers as well as being in the midst of amazing animals, Adam was not fulfilled or complete. *"But for Adam there was not found an help meet for him"* (Genesis 2:20). An *help meet* is that which fits perfectly and is suitable. Something was missing for Adam. God said, *"It is not good"* (Genesis 2:18a).

Though placed in a beautiful garden with enjoyable and exciting work, alongside the scores of animals who were without ferociousness, Adam was alone. Within the heart of Adam, the loving Lord God created the desire for closeness and connection. Thus, in an incredible surgical procedure, God took living tissue from the spot that was very near Adam's heart. From this the Scriptures reveal, "...*Made he a woman, and brought her unto the man*" (Genesis 2:22).

God brought Eve to Adam. In a very beautiful and dramatic way, when Adam opened his eyes, the Lord personally presented Eve to her husband. She became his "help meet" in that Adam now was complete.

In what ways do you already see your role as an "help meet" to your future mate? _____

_____

The First Bridal Couple

What must have gone through the mind and heart of Adam when the Lord brought Eve to him? There must have been a sense of supreme joy and amazement in the precious and beautiful provision of the Lord. Moses notes, in the context of the marriage in Eden, four essential elements of a successful marriage. This is a review from counseling session one. Your counselor may ask you how the following material has affected your conviction throughout the counseling process.

Severance
"*Therefore shall a man leave his father and his mother*" (Genesis 2:24a). The idea of *leaving* is a picture of one untying a shoestring. That which formerly bound us in the child-parent relationship now is loosened or unbound. It is not that a man deserts his father or mother. Rather, he is no longer bound to his parents as when he was a child.

Permanence
"*And shall cleave unto his wife*" (Genesis 2:24b). The word *cleave* is a strong word. It denotes the act of becoming glued, so permanently bonded to another that the bond cannot be broken without great and lasting damage.

It will be important to emphasize once again that marriage is not a contract. Contracts are written in such a way as to provide for loopholes, conditional clauses, and ultimately how to get out of an obligation. Marriage is actually a covenant. The Old Testament Prophet Malachi testified in the strongest of terms to husbands who were sinning. He declared, *"The LORD hath been witness between thee and the wife of thy youth, against whom thou hast dealt treacherously: yet is she thy companion, and the wife of thy covenant"* (Malachi 2:14).

In a covenant, couples pledge to each other their lives. There are no provisions for loopholes or clauses to get out of the agreement. Some of the old marriage services actually use the phrase "I plight thee my troth." Most today would have no idea what a troth plighted would be! A *plighted troth* is a solemn pledge or promise.

Adam became glued to his wife. That is intimacy. Married couples grow in intimacy by understanding the permanence of pledging their lives to another and becoming glued to that person.

Closeness
"And they shall be one flesh" (Genesis 2:24c). One flesh speaks of a unity, closeness, and a bond that embraces the emotional, physical, and sexual realms. Rather than living under the terms of "me and I," the one flesh couple develops the "we and us" mentality and lifestyle. This comes with good communication, honesty and integrity, time shared, reaching common values and convictions, as well as building the marriage upon the Lord Himself.

Intimacy
"And they were both naked, the man and his wife, and were not ashamed" (Genesis 2:25). The concept of not being ashamed contains two elements. First, they were not embarrassed; second, they were not disappointed. The love Adam and Eve shared with each other was beautifully expressed in Genesis 4:1 with the expression *"Adam knew Eve his wife."* The sexual intercourse of Adam and Eve demonstrated their emotional and spiritual closeness as well as the joy shared physically with each other.

The Creator God gave Adam and Eve, as well as married couples throughout the generations, the same beautiful expression of intimacy.

Sexual expression within the boundaries of the marriage of the man and woman is part of God's design.

Healthy Sexual Expression

God has clearly designed men and women to find great fulfillment and satisfaction through the intensely intimate connection of sexuality.

1. Within the boundaries of marriage, sexual love is a gift from God and is therefore honorable (Hebrews 13:4).

2. Sex is not to be selfishly sought for one's own pleasure; rather it is given as a token and demonstration of love for one's partner.

3. Sexual activity is intended to bring fulfillment and satisfaction to both partners. Therefore it is not to be given as a reward, nor is it to be withheld as punishment.

4. As the fulfillment of a closeness being built into the marriage, wise couples must talk about their sexual experience. The husband and wife who share a healthy concept of their sexuality understand that the act of marriage requires practice and patience with each other. This is especially true during the early days and weeks of your marriage.

Eager anticipation and desire continue to grow throughout your engagement. Wise and godly couples build extra safeguards into their relationship as their wedding approaches. The temptation to "Go ahead and have some fun. You will be married soon" grows very strong in these days. Wait until you are married! It is well worth the wait, and you will be glad you made the wise decision.

What if you are already sexually active? It is impossible to roll time backwards and undo that which has already taken place. Confess and acknowledge this to the Lord. Forgive each other, and forgive yourself. Commit to each other and to the Lord that you will immediately stop any and all sexual activity until your wedding night. Ask the Lord to help you grow in grace and determination.

While anticipation and excitement grow, often apprehension does as well. Fear of the unknown, fear of failure, and fear that you will somehow be a disappointment to your mate often are typical feelings of couples as they approach their wedding. Ask the Lord to help you with your fears. Talk with your future mate about your fears, and be willing to talk with your counselor about this.

The wife has the need to be loved and cherished. She is aroused much more slowly (some would suggest it begins in the kitchen as the husband helps with dishes!) and needs time to prepare for the bedroom. Physical touch and tender words prepare her for intimacy.

Quite the opposite, the man is aroused by thought and sight. He is ready for intimacy much more quickly than his wife. Both partners must understand their mate and desire to be thoughtful, caring, loving, and sexually giving in their marriage. Godly husbands must learn to be gentle, loving, affectionate, and demonstrative in cherishing their wives. On the other hand, a godly wife knows her husband has very strong sexual drives. She loves her husband and is thankful she can express her love for him, and she finds joy in freely giving herself to him.

Healthy sexual attitudes are built upon the fact that the couple no longer have claim to their own bodies. Rather, in love and tenderness, both give their bodies to each other (1 Corinthians 7:4). In the mutual giving, there is mutual satisfaction.

Even if you do not enjoy reading, it will be very wise for you and your future mate to separately read several books that deal with the gift of sexuality from a biblical perspective. Among the many possibilities (without full recommendation or endorsement of the author) would be these books:

- *The Honeymoon of Your Dreams* by Walt Larimore and Susan Crockett, Regal Books, 2005.
- *The Act of Marriage* by Tim and Beverly LaHaye, Zondervan Publishing House, 1998.
- *Intended for Pleasure* by Ed and Gayle Wheat, Fleming H. Revell Publishers, 1997.

Work on this section during your counseling session

Your pastor-counselor will share with you and your future mate several very important principles relating to intimacy. It will be important to ask questions if there is something that you do not understand. Be ready to fill in several blanks and jot down additional notes in the margins during this session.

My Personal Notes from this Counseling Session

Danger! Intimacy Can Be Damaged and Destroyed!

Intimacy is much more than just sexual intercourse. While sex is great, the whole concept of intimacy is far greater. Intimacy is the closeness that results from a couple being glued together emotionally as well as sexually.

Within every marriage, dangers ahead lurk nearby which consistently threaten the closeness and intimacy of marriage. While the following is not an exhaustive list, these are the typical dangers that damage and destroy marriages.

_____ not fulfilled

An expectation is that which is established in the mind of a person as to certainties or demands. Looking forward, an expectation is something that person surely anticipates and toward which he or she is looking. While some expectations are reasonable, many are not. Several common but not realistic expectations in marriage would include the following:

- My husband is not only going to love me; he will be romantic every day in the way he treats me.
- My wife is going to cook for me just exactly like my mother cooks.
- My husband is going to appreciate all my efforts and will tell me often how special I am.
- My wife will always be ready for sex when I suggest it.
- My husband will be thoughtful of my feelings and will speak tenderly to me even when he is frustrated.
- My wife will always respect my leadership and will encourage me even when I am having a hard day.

- My husband will tell me about all the details of his day. He will love to share with me at length about everything.
- My wife will understand that I want a little quietness and relaxation without talking all evening long.

Why are these expectations not realistic? _____

_____

Don't be surprised if your counselor asks you to share some of your expectations. While not limited to this list, these things will provide a good beginning to understanding expectations. When not fulfilled, a wedge is created and closeness is damaged.

_____ not fulfilled

Emergencies can unexpectedly change the best-laid plans, in a great hurry! There is a big difference between the infrequent emergency and the consistently broken promise that shatters intimacy.

Ultimately, the Lord Himself is the only one who has never broken a promise (1 Kings 8:56). Promises fulfilled are not only the rule of a healthy marriage, they are the characteristic of genuine Christianity (Romans 12:17). Broken promises relating to dates, activities, shared experiences and family living create huge wedges that destroy closeness.

_____ not resolved

Think of it. You and your future mate are two people, living independently of each other for several decades, coming from different backgrounds, with different personalities and different preferences, uniting to form a relationship that is characterized by "one flesh" in nature. Conflicts are inevitable. Unresolved conflicts grow and can fester, resulting in serious damage to the closeness of the marriage. The following are among the typically unresolved conflicts that damage intimacy.

- How frequently do we hope to have sexual activity in the week?
- Who will handle the checkbook and how we will spend our money?
- How soon will we start our family?
- How often will we visit each other's family?
- What are the things we really need in our home?

- How many children do we wish to raise?
- What are the duties we want our mate to fulfill?
- How do we want our home to be kept, and how do we want it to look?
- How much should we save and put away for emergencies and retirement?
- What will we do in our leisure time?
- How will she know she is cherished?
- How will he know he is respected?
- Will both couples work after the baby comes?

_____ not wisely managed

Most couples are busy; many are too busy. If there is not sufficient time for worship, work, service, recreation, and family, that schedule is overloaded. Overloaded schedules rob couples of intimacy!

Time management is better understood as the wise handling of God's stewardship of time. The Lord owns or possesses everything, including time. As stewards, you must be faithful in the way you manage time and handle the many potential activities that come (1 Corinthians 4:2).

Intimate couples who enjoy a growing closeness give first priority to the Lord Jesus. He is the object of worship, praise, and obedience to the godly couple. Worship comes first in the daily priority of wise time management.

Even though work is a major activity in the stewardship of time, it must never become the idol demanding more and more allegiance and investment. A huge and dangerous trap to be avoided by those couples who grow in intimacy is the overly demanding pressure and temptation to expend undue time to accumulate more riches. Those who set riches as the ultimate priority open themselves to great harm and hurt (1 Timothy 6:6-10).

Family time provides the opportunity to reconnect after a busy day in the work world. Though most couples need a few minutes of quietness and personal time, wise couples enjoy being together, talking with each other, playing together and sharing experiences together even in the very common and routine matters such as running errands. This is called *connection* and is a necessary component of emotional intimacy.

_____ **that are not thoughtful**

In many ways, marriage is very much like a bank. Every action that is helpful, blessed, encouraging, and uplifting is similar to making a deposit in the bank. Likewise the thoughtless or hurtful action, which should be very infrequent, is comparable to making withdrawals from the bank. Obviously, healthy bank accounts have many more deposits than withdrawals. The same is true in marriages.

A careful reading of 1 Corinthians 13 clearly defines actions that are loving, thoughtful, and kind. The couple who would enjoy intimacy in marriage are those who live out the description of the Apostle as he wrote to the Corinthian believers. Imagine the closeness in marriage that comes when husbands and wives are committed to the following principles from 1 Corinthians 13:

- Love is patient
- Love is kind
- Love does not envy
- Love does not boast
- Love is not proud
- Love is not rude
- Love is not self-seeking
- Love is not easily angered
- Love keeps no record or lists of wrong doing
- Love does not delight in evil, but rejoices with the truth
- Love always protects and trusts
- Love hopes and perseveres
- Love never fails

There will be many additional thoughts and principles your pastor-counselor may wish to add at this point.

Additional Notes from this Counseling Session

_____

_____

_____

_____

It is wise for the bride to schedule a gynecological visit. While it is rare, occasionally she may require a minor surgical procedure. Certainly if the bride is going to use birth control methods requiring a prescription, such an appointment will be necessary. Be sure in the appointment to be very clear with the physician that you desire to prevent pregnancy, not terminate it.

There is nothing as precious as the couple who experiences the intimate blessing of the Song of Solomon 2:16, "My beloved is mine, and I am his."

Planning Your Special Day

The day is approaching! There will never be another day like this one. Before the Lord God and the witness of your family and friends, you will stand and enter a lifelong covenant with your beloved partner for life. Next to the day when you placed your trust in Christ for salvation, this, no doubt, is the most significant day of your life. Previous chapters had areas in which the couple was requested to work before the counseling session. This session is unique in that it has no required work before your appointment!

Work on this section during your counseling session

There are several very important questions to answer honestly as your wedding day approaches. Your pastor will work through these with you.

1. Do you as a couple possess a strong testimony of personal faith in the Lord Jesus? What is discernible about your spiritual growth? _____

   _____

2. Does the groom demonstrate the characteristics of being a godly, loving, spiritual leader? What are several such characteristics he consistently (not perfectly!) demonstrates? _____

   _____

   Does the bride demonstrate the characteristics of being a godly, loving wife? What are several such characteristics she consistently (not perfectly!) demonstrates? _____

   _____

3. What areas of potential conflict that surfaced in earlier premarital counseling are being addressed and resolved? _____

_____

4. Are both families happy with the upcoming wedding? If not, what are their concerns? _____

_____

Has any situation developed that you should share with your pastor?

_____

_____

5. Are there any other questions or concerns that must be addressed?

_____

These must be addressed with the pastor-counselor. Perhaps he will wish to schedule another session with you as a couple.

There are several wonderful things to consider as you plan your wedding with the pastor in this seventh counseling session.

A Godly Wedding Ceremony

In a wonderful way, Christ adorned the wedding at Cana (John 2) with his personal presence. Here is a great reminder. As you begin your new life together and establish your godly home, commit to making your wedding and reception (which will be discussed in a later chapter) a God-honoring and glorifying celebration. Several things to keep in mind in establishing a godly wedding and reception would include the following:

1. Often unsaved family and friends attend the believer's wedding when otherwise they would not likely attend a preaching service. A great opportunity for planting an evangelistic seed is possible in the godly wedding. You have a great opportunity to seize this occasion to lovingly present the gospel clearly.

2. Your pastor will tactfully and tenderly filter out items that are not biblical or godly. Select wisely and carefully the special music. Do not be surprised if the pastor wishes to know and review your desired musical selections as well as any special readings, poems, or personally-written parts of the ceremony. Though it is your wedding, it is important to remember that the pastor is in charge and must make the final approval on every aspect of the wedding and reception.

3. If you wish to use a ceremony different from what the pastor will offer, graciously understand he must read it as soon as possible. Very few couples are writers. Most will not desire to write their own ceremony. However, if you do wish to write the vows, your pastor may find it necessary to help you rethink and reword some of your statements.

4. This is a celebration of two families who love their children and are coming together before the Lord and the presence of friends to witness the establishment of a godly home and family. You as a couple are not entering a contract; but rather a covenant and companionship (Malachi 2:14). The vows are significant and must be highlighted and emphasized. For these to be established, you must genuinely seek the Lord and invite Him to be part of the entire day.

With this in view, this chapter will present you and the counselor with a suggested form to be completed to list all the wedding details. Also several wedding ceremonies written by the author are available to be used for your wedding ceremony, if you so desire.

This day is so important that you must earnestly determine to make your wedding a godly testimony and beautiful celebration that will be pleasing to the Lord Jesus, a blessing to all who attend, and a day in which you both will remember and rejoice on your journey of a lifetime.

Wedding Details for the Couple and Pastor

Note: Check with your pastor as to when he requires this form to be submitted. Some pastors prefer to have this before the session. Other pastors complete this form in the counseling session with the couple present.

Groom's full name _____

Bride's full name _____

Date of wedding _____ Time _____

Maid/Matron of Honor _____

Maids attending: _____

_____

_____

Best Man _____

Ushers: _____

_____

_____

Flower Girl _____

Ring Bearer _____

Organist _____

Special music _____

_____

Wedding service selected _____

Wedding Coordinator _____

Florist _____

Photographer _____

Date of wedding rehearsal _____ Time _____

Approximate number attending wedding _____

Special features to be included in the ceremony _____

_____

_____

Master of Ceremonies at reception _____

Should you use a wedding coordinator?

Based on Ephesians 4:12, pastors are to labor tirelessly in equipping the saints for ministry. Godly pastors do not function alone in performing ministry. Rather, biblical pastors help and train believers to do the work of the ministry.

One such ministry is that of the wedding coordinator. Many a pastor has experienced the feelings of being frazzled as he, the groom, and the ushers nervously stand in an adjacent room up in the front of the auditorium wondering what was happening, awaiting the delayed beginning of the wedding. At precisely 1:00 the organist was supposed to play "O Perfect Love" signifying the candles were lit and the bride was ready. It is now 1:07 and no "O Perfect Love!" What does the pastor do now? His options are to peek out the door, walk down a side aisle trying to act like this is part of the plan, or just wait it out with the anxious groom and his attendants. None of those options is pleasant.

A wedding coordinator can be of great benefit not only in getting everyone in the right place at the right time, but also in assisting the pastor with many details of the wedding and ceremony. Professional wedding coordinators are hired to be in charge and carry out the wishes and contractual agreement with the bride (and her parents, who are paying for the wedding). The professionally-hired coordinator operates within the budget and secures all the venues of the wedding, including the church and minister. In this sense, most godly couples will not plan a gala wedding that costs tens of thousands of dollars and therefore will not find it necessary to expend such a sum of money on a professional coordinator.

The pastor must be in charge of the ceremony, facilities, and activities. However, wise pastors have found great benefits and rewards in training at least one willing lady to serve as wedding coordinator. If your pastor offers you the service of a church wedding coordinator, it may be wise to seriously consider his suggestion.

The ministry responsibilities of the biblical wedding coordinator would include, but are not limited to the following:

1. The Wedding Coordinator (WC) will be contacted by either the bride or pastor at least four months before the wedding date to ensure that she is available on the date selected for the wedding.

2. The WC will meet with the bride (and possibly the mother of the bride) to review the details of the wedding and reception. The WC will advise the bride and give suggestions that will help the wedding ceremony and reception to function smoothly.

3. The WC will work closely with the bride and her family, being available to supervise the setting up of the reception as well as being the point person for the florist, photographer, wedding cake baker, caterer, video technician, sound room technician, and attendants. She oversees the arrival of the wedding attendants, the changing rooms, floral arrangements, guest book placement, and double-checks on the special arrangements of the wedding ceremony.

4. In most local church weddings, the bride's family will enlist help to set up for the reception as well as the cleanup that follows. The WC will be available to make suggestions or offer help with these details.

5. The WC will assist the pastor in the rehearsal of the ceremony. Each pastor will decide how much of the responsibility of the wedding rehearsal will fall to the WC. Some pastors prefer being in charge of the rehearsal with the WC being primarily responsible for ensuring the bridal party is lined up and ready for the ceremony at the appointed time.

   Other pastors prefer to have the WC oversee more of the rehearsal. While the pastor is in attendance and will rehearse the wedding ceremony with the couple, in this case the WC will rehearse with the attendants the role of the ushers, the placement in the processional as well as in the ceremony, the coordinating of the preliminary music, and the details such as lighting of the candles, extending the runner, and possible special music before the wedding ceremony begins.

6. Even if the pastor prefers not to enlist and train a WC, it is advisable to have a trusted and administrative lady to be in the back of the auditorium with the bridal party to ensure that all members are ready

for the ceremony to begin. This will relieve much of the pressure on both the pastor and you as the bridal couple on the day of your wedding.

Wedding ceremonies available to be used

You have permission to use any of these samples as written. If an officiating pastor wishes to rewrite any portion of these samples, please contact Dr. Michael Peck at Baptist Church Planters for permission. Special features may be added without seeking the author's permission.

The next chapter will present possible special features to consider for your wedding. Here are several ceremonies to consider in your wedding.

Wedding Ceremony Sample 1

The Processional

What a wonderful God to whom we believers belong! He is referred to by many names and characteristics in the Bible. Perhaps the most beautiful of all His names is the personal name, Yahweh, Jehovah. This is the amazing personal name that means He is the self-existent One, the eternal God Himself. Unlike His creation, our God is self-sufficient. He needs no one else to survive and to exist. Yet, incredibly, in eternity past, the Father, Son and Holy Spirit made a beautiful and incredibly amazing decision. They would reveal themselves and create man.

Thus into the beautiful flowers of the Garden of Eden, God created and placed Adam, the first man. Adam the man was the crown of all God's creation. He was given the garden to explore, dress and keep for the Lord. Work was to be totally enjoyable there in the beautiful, weedless, sinless garden. Adam also enjoyed the friendship of the animals. With no ferociousness, Adam sensed no fear as he mingled with the incredible animal kingdom. Most amazing of all, Adam must have sensed great joy as he experienced the fellowship of Jehovah God.

Yet dear friends, something was missing. The Bible records the Lord's statement in Genesis 2:18, "It is not good that the man should be alone; I will make him an help meet for him." God already knew that something was missing in Adam's life. He gave Adam the opportunity and time to make such a discovery for himself. Hence, God performed the first surgery and removed living tissue from the side of Adam. This tissue was not from his head to rule over her, nor from his feet to trample her under; but from his side. This tissue was taken from the spot closest to the heart of Adam, his very rib. This demonstrates that Eve was to be close to him. At his side, beautifully equal in value, she was to be cherished and loved. She was his companion, his help meet.

As Adam awoke from the surgery, a beautiful sight awaited him as recorded in Genesis 2:22. The Bible declares that God brought her unto the man. Adam's first moments of consciousness must have been joyous. Now he had a sweet addition to his formerly lonely life; Eve was the cherished partner of God's choosing.

Today before this assembled congregation, another reenactment of the Lord's working is taking place as He brings (<u>Bride's name</u>) and (<u>Groom's name</u>) together in marriage. It is special to remember that God Himself officiated at the first of all the wedding ceremonies. He blessed the marriage of Adam and Eve with His own presence. Likewise today, the Lord is here with us and earnestly desires to bless this marriage and home.

Prayer

Counsel

    Counsel to the Groom: (<u>Groom's name</u>), as Adam was not fulfilled apart from Eve, so you will never find true fulfillment apart from (<u>Bride's name</u>). Not only is your wedding a picture of what the Lord did in the garden of Eden, even greater it is a vivid picture of the relationship between Christ and His church. When you love your wife as the Bible commands, you will love her even as Christ loved the church and gave Himself for it. While you may never have the opportunity of laying down your life for your wife, you certainly can live for her each day. May Christ Himself aide and assist you in becoming the kind of husband He wants you to be. (<u>Groom's name</u>), may you be strong of character, deep in courage, consistent in conviction, great in tenderness, and excellent in your devoted love and considerate treatment of your wife. She is God's precious gift to you.

Counsel to the Bride: (Brides' name), as Eve was brought to Adam long ago to be his help meet, may you find a great sense of joy in your role as partner, friend, counselor, lover and encourager. A help meet is one that is just right, perfectly suitable for her partner. Thus, may the Lord give you a special love and respect for your husband. The submission of the wife as commanded in the Scriptures is not the submission of dread and fear; but of love, joy and respect. Make your husband your best friend and serve the Lord together as partners. May you be godly in character, faithful in living, and gracious in your love for Christ and your husband.

Presentation of the Bride

To the Father: Dad, what a special time for you and your wife. The years of training, nurturing and teaching bring you to this joyous moment. Do you and your wife this day present your daughter to be married to this man? **Father replies, "Yes, her mother and I do."** (Father kisses daughter and shakes the hand of the groom as he welcomes him into his family. Father is seated.)

The Vows

To the Groom: (Groom's name), before the Lord I am now asking you in the presence of these witnesses, do you willingly and joyfully take (Bride's name) to be your own precious wife? Do you promise this day that you will love her, honor her, protect her, cherish her, and give yourself always to your wife, as a godly husband should? **Groom replies, "I do."**

To the Bride: (Bride's name), before the Lord I am now asking you in the presence of these witnesses, do you willingly and joyfully take (Groom's name) to be your own precious husband? Do you promise this day that you will love him, honor him, and cherish him, even as a godly wife should? **Bride replies, "I do."**

At this point if the bride is carrying a floral arrangement, she will pass it to her maid/matron of honor.

To the Couple: You have promised that you are joyfully taking each other as husband and wife. Would you now join your right hands? The beautiful symbolism of the right hand in the Old Testament demonstrated strength and might. Today as you join your right hands, you are joining together in a new and beautiful strength.

These vows are for a lifetime. The promises you are making are unconditional. Together you are pledging your lives in a loving covenant of strength and beauty. Malachi 2:14 states "she is your companion and the wife of your covenant."

To the Groom: (The groom turns and faces his bride to repeat his vows.) Please repeat your vows after me. "I (Groom's name) take you (Bride's name)... to be my own... wedded wife. I love you... with all of my heart... and I pledge to you... that I will seek... to become the husband... God wants me to be. I cherish you... and commit myself to you. This commitment is for better or worse... richer or poorer... in sickness and in health... as long as life shall last. I pledge to you... my life and love."

To the Bride: (The bride still facing her groom to repeat her vows.) Please repeat your vows after me. "I (Bride's name) take you (Groom's name) ...to be my own... wedded husband. I love you... with all of my heart. I pledge to you... I will seek to become... the wife God wants me to be. I cherish you... and commit myself to you. This commitment is for better or worse... richer or poorer... in sickness and in health... as long as life shall last. I pledge to you... my life and love."

The Exchanging of the Rings

The vows just repeated are both beautiful and lasting. (Groom's name) and (Bride's name) have pledged to each other their life and love. Now we come to the moment in the ceremony where the rings are placed on the ring finger of the bride and groom. These rings are the outward and visible symbol of the vows just repeated. Daily the couple will see their wedding rings and will be reminded of this very special moment when they pledged to each other their life and love.

To the Groom: (Groom's name), please place the ring on your bride's ring finger and repeat after me, "I place this ring... on your finger... to constantly remind you... of the love I have for you... and the promise of my life. With this ring... I marry you today."

To the Bride: (Bride's name), please place the ring on your groom's ring finger and repeat after me, "I place this ring… on your finger… to constantly remind you… of the love I have for you… and the promise of my life. With this ring… I marry you today."

The Pronouncement

For as much then, as you (Groom's full name and Bride's full name) have joyfully entered this marriage and have pledged your total commitment to each other, I therefore by the authority vested in me as a minister of the Lord Jesus Christ, pronounce you husband and wife.

The Lord Jesus Himself said, "What therefore God has joined together, let no man put asunder" according to Matthew 19:6. (Groom's name and Bride's name), let no difficulty, no disappointment, no obstacle ever divide you asunder. Do not allow any person to come between you. May the love you have for each other this day continue to grow and blossom. As the Lord allows, may you have many years together and may you have the joy of growing old together. May the peace of Christ and the joy of the Lord mark your home. The Psalmist of old declared in Psalm 128:1, "Blessed is every one that feareth the LORD; that walketh in his ways."

May the Lord bless you and keep you. May the Lord make His face to shine upon you and be gracious unto you. May the Lord give you joy and peace as you walk with Him each day.

Prayer

The husband may now kiss his wife.

The Presentation

(The couple turns and faces the congregation as the bride takes her floral arrangement once again.) Now, it is my very happy privilege to introduce and present to you, Mr. and Mrs. (Name).

The Recessional

Wedding Ceremony Sample 2

The Processional

The Welcome

Dear family and friends of (Groom's name) and dear family and friends of (Bride's name) we come together today to celebrate this very special moment. It is our privilege to hear the vows they will make to each other as well as witness the giving and receiving of the wedding rings. We will share in the joy of the pronouncement of their marriage. On behalf of the bride and groom, welcome and thank you for sharing in this most joyous occasion.

Marriage, home and family are God's idea and plan. In the beautiful Garden of Eden, God brought Eve to Adam to be his help meet, his companion, and his completion. Christ Himself performed his first miracle at the wedding of Cana. The Apostle Paul declared marriage to be honorable. The home was God's very first institution. We come today with joy and excitement as we share this very special occasion with two people we love. Let us begin the service with prayer and ask the Lord's blessing.

Prayer

Charge to the Couple

(Groom's name and Bride's name), it is a blessing to gather today to celebrate your marriage. This day marks a new beginning in your lives. A brand-new home will be established in the next few moments. The Lord has wonderfully worked in your lives and brought you together for a lifetime. You are about to exchange vows that are best understood as the pledging of your life. These vows are not contracts which can be broken or renegotiated. Rather, you are entering a covenant, a lifelong pledge of giving yourselves to each other. This marriage covenant is for a lifetime. The Lord wants to bless your marriage and home with his grace and help.

The Presentation

To the Father: Dad, you and your wife rejoiced when your daughter was born. As parents, you taught her to walk. Then you taught her to ride a bicycle. Next you taught her to drive a car. Probably the years have flown by very quickly for you. Now your life enters the next dimension as you bring your daughter to this man to be his wife. Is it your intention this day to give your daughter in marriage to this man? **Father replies, "Yes, her mother and I do."** (Father kisses daughter and shakes hand of groom welcoming him to his family. Father is seated.)

The Vows

No other ties compare to the bonding as husband and wife. No other vows are more significant than what you are about to make. The Lord Jesus Christ and your family and friends rejoice in what you are about to promise.

To the Groom: (Groom's name), do you this day take this woman to become your own wedded wife? Do you promise to establish a home that is godly, and do you promise to live with your wife as a loving spiritual leader who is pleasing to the Lord? Do you promise to love her, cherish her, provide for her and protect her? Do you pledge to her your love and life? **Groom replies, "I do."**

To the Bride: (Bride's name), do you this day take this man to become your own wedded husband? Do you promise to establish a home that is godly, and do you promise to live with your husband as a loving spiritual wife? Do you promise to love him, cherish him, serve with him as his partner and be a wife that is pleasing to the Lord? Do you pledge to him your love and life? **Bride replies, "I do."**

The Reading of Ephesians 5:21-33

(A greeting from the bridal couple, either from the groom himself or by the pastor on their behalf followed by a brief presentation of the gospel is appropriate at this point in the service.)

I will now ask the bride and groom to face each other and hold their hands. (If the bride is carrying a floral arrangement, she will pass it to the maid/matron of honor.) You have indicated your desire to become husband and wife. The Song of Solomon 2:16 declares, "My beloved is mine, and I am his…" This speaks of oneness, closeness and a joy in knowing you belong to each other. These vows you are about to make are the pledges of your lifetime.

To the Groom: (Groom's name), you will repeat your vows after me, "I (Groom's name) take you (Bride's name)… to be my wedded wife. I pledge my life to you… to have and to hold… from this day forward. I freely give my love to you… in days that are better or worse… times when we are richer or poorer… in cases of sickness or health… for the rest of my life. I pledge this to you… as your own husband."

To the Bride: (Bride's name), you will repeat your vows after me, "I (Bride's name) take you (Groom's name) … to be my wedded husband. I pledge my life to you… to have and to hold…from this day forward. I freely give my love to you… in days that are better or worse… times when we are richer or poorer… in cases of sickness or health… for the rest of my life. I pledge this to you… as your own wife."

The Exchanging of the Rings

The wedding ring is a beautiful symbol of the vows that were just exchanged. Every day the couple will see their rings and remember once again what they have promised. The wedding ring displayed announces that I belong to another. My life is no longer my own. I am married and have pledge my life, love and loyalty to my beloved.

To the Groom: You will repeat after me as you place the ring upon the bride's ring finger. "With this ring… I now marry you… and pledge to you… my constant trust… and abiding love."

To the Bride: You will repeat after me as you place the ring upon the groom's ring finger. "With this ring… I now marry you… and pledge to you… my constant trust… and abiding love."

May these rings given and received be the constant reminder of your love and devotion to each other and may the Lord abundantly bless your marriage.

The Pronouncement

For as much as (<u>Groom's full name</u>) and (<u>Bride's full name</u>) have consented to marriage and have confirmed this by declaring it in vows and exchanging of wedding rings, by the authority committed unto me as a minister of the Lord Jesus Christ and the State of (<u>name of state</u>), I now therefore pronounce you husband and wife.

Closing Charge

Dearly beloved, this day marks a brand new beginning in your lives now united. You are no longer single. No longer is it me, myself and I. Now today marks the start of the journey of a lifetime as husband and wife. The words "us" and "we" will become the new normal. Keep Christ first in your lives, marriage and home. Seek His blessing in every thing you do. Ask His direction in every decision ahead. Make Him the Lord of your household. May the desire of your heart be the same as Joshua as he declared, "But as for me and my house, we will serve the Lord" (Joshua 24:15).

Prayer

(<u>Groom's name</u>) you may now kiss your new wife.

Presentation and Introduction

(Minister suggests that the couple turn and face the congregation. Bride takes her floral arrangement from the maid/matron of honor). Families and friends, it is now my joyous privilege to introduce and present to you, Mr. and Mrs. (<u>full name</u>).

Recessional

Wedding Ceremony Sample 3

The Processional

The Welcome

Dear family and friends, on behalf of (<u>names of Groom and Bride</u>) I would like to welcome you and thank you for coming today. What an incredible day this is to this dear couple as well as to the Lord Jesus Christ, to the parents of the bride and groom and to each of you as family and friends.

As the seasons of the year come and go, likewise there are seasons in our lives. To the parents, it probably seems like such a short time ago you held your babies in your arms as you dreamed of what their lives would be like. You saw them take their first really wobbly steps. When they skinned their knee, you were there to kiss it and make it all better.

You taught them how to ride a bike, skip a stone across the water, and make a kite. Before you knew it, kindergarten came, and you couldn't believe it when they graduated from high school. Now today, you are part of a very great day in their lives. Two individual people, uniquely designed by an all-wise and loving Lord, each with their own distinct personalities, backgrounds, and talents, come to be united in marriage.

The Bible says in Genesis 2:24 and 25, "Therefore shall a man leave his father and his mother, and shall cleave unto his wife: and they shall be one flesh. And they were both naked, the man and his wife, and were not ashamed." Modern day philosophy says, "I am the most important person in the whole world. I deserve to be happy, and therefore my great purpose is to please myself." But for the believing couple, the greatest joy in all of life is together seeking to please the Lord and love one another for a lifetime.

This love is a very special love. It is called *agape* love. The Lord Jesus said, "Greater love hath no man than this, that a man lay down his life for his friends" (John 15:13). This love is a decision of your will, that you will consistently and devotedly seek the well-being of the other. Such love will bring joy to your home and blessing to your lives. This kind of love will face the greatest adversities, resolve the deepest conflicts, and survive the greatest storms. When you as a couple love one another and become one flesh, home will be a blessing and your marriage will be precious. This love will deepen as you grow older together.

To the Father: Dad, the little girl you held in your arms is now a beautiful lady. Is it the intention of you and your wife to bring your daughter to this man for marriage today? **Father replies, "Her mother and I**

give our blessing." Father kisses his daughter, shakes the hand of the groom, and joins them in the aisle before being seated.

Today is a blending of that which is a celebration and that which is sacred and serious. We celebrate the goodness of God and His precious provision of each for the other. As family and friends, we share together many wonderful and often humorous experiences. The reception will be a time marked with remembering and rejoicing.

On the other hand, this couple is about to pledge to each other their lives. This moment marks the solemn and lifelong commitment to one another. (Names of Groom and Bride), you are entering into the making of a lifelong covenant. You are pledging to each other a mutual trust and devotion, never to be shared with another as long as life shall last. We are witnesses together of this precious and powerful moment.

To the Groom: (Name of Groom), do you realize what a treasure you have been given by the Lord? The writer of Proverbs states, "Who can find a virtuous woman? for her price is far above rubies" (Proverbs 31:10). When you view your wife as a treasure far above the value of rubies, you then begin to understand the gift God has given to you. Treasure her. Thank the Lord for her. Be to her a godly husband. When you love your wife in the same manner as Christ loves His church, your life will never be the same. Such love in your heart will help you to determine to be the loving, gentle and godly spiritual leader in your home. Such love will help you through any situation. May God bless your role of husband. May you live in such a way as to never violate the trust your wife has in you.

To the Bride: Throughout the Scriptures, precious ladies have found great joy and blessing in being united to their husbands and lovingly them tenderly and devotedly. Of Eve, the Scriptures record that God brought her unto the man. Imagine the joy and anticipation Rebekah had when the Scriptures speak of her becoming Isaac's wife and his love for her. Over and over the love story is repeated. Ruth and Boaz, Abigail and David, Mary and Joseph are among the many. Today you join a precious company of godly ladies blessed by the Lord and loved by their husbands. May God bless your role of wife. May you live in such a way as to never violate the trust your husband has in you.

Prayer

Scripture: Matthew 19:5-6

The Vows

This moment marks the pledging of each other for a lifetime. Far beyond a contract which can be broken and renegotiated, this covenant pledges the lives of the husband and wife to each as long as life lasts.

(The minister suggests the bride give her floral arrangement to the maid/matron of honor, and the couple turns, facing each other and holding hands.)

To the Groom: (Name of Groom), if it is your intention to enter into the marriage vows, then you will repeat the following after me. "I (Name of Groom) rejoice in God's blessing... and His gift to me. I pledge my love and life... to you (Name of Bride)... and will be faithful to you... honor and love you...protect and cherish you... as long as life shall last. I give to you... the pledge of my love... in days of sickness and health... days of being richer or poorer... for better or worse. I am yours."

To the Bride: (Name of Bride), if it is your intention to enter into the marriage vows, then you will repeat the following after me. "I (Name of Bride) rejoice in God's blessing... and His gift to me. I pledge my love and life... to you (Name of Groom)... and will be faithful to you... I will honor and love you... and keep myself only for you... as long as life shall last. I give to you... the pledge of my love... in days of sickness and health... days of being richer or poorer... for better or worse. I am yours."

The Exchanging of the Rings

This couple has entered into a lifelong covenant together. We are witnesses of these joyous vows. Now comes the exchanging of the rings which is the outward, visible symbol of the promise just made.

To the Groom: (Name of Groom), you will place the ring on your bride's ring finger and repeat the following after me. "(Name of Bride), I give you this ring... as the token of my pledge. May it constantly remind us... of our promise and joy. I take you as my precious wife."

To the Bride: (<u>Name of Bride</u>), you will place the ring on your groom's ring finer and repeat the following after me. "(<u>Name of Groom</u>), I give you this ring… as the token of my pledge. May it constantly remind us… of our promise and joy. I take you as my precious husband."

The Pronouncement

Today (<u>Groom's full name</u>) and (<u>Bride's full name</u>) have presented themselves before this company of witnesses and have each pledged their lives to the other. They have exchanged rings as visible tokens of this enduring pledge. Therefore, by the authority vested in me as a minister of the Lord Jesus Christ and by the State of _____, I now pronounce you to be husband and wife. What God has joined together, let no man divide asunder.

Closing Benediction

A brand-new home has just been established. May the joy of the presence of Christ, the authority of the Word of God and the fellowship that comes when two people are devoted to the Lord characterize your lives. May your home be godly. May your lives grow closer to each other and to the Lord who dearly loves you both. May the Lord bless and keep you in the days and years ahead.

(<u>Name of Groom</u>) you may now kiss your new wife.

Introduction and Presentation

(The minister now suggests the couple turn and face the congregation as the bride takes her floral arrangement from the maid/matron of honor.) Now it is my very happy privilege to introduce and present to you, Mr. and Mrs. (<u>Name</u>).

Recessional

****

May the Lord give you wisdom in selecting the wedding ceremony as well as grace as you work with your pastor-counselor. At times, various individuals will share their opinions and suggestions at the wedding rehearsal. If you are receiving lots of suggestions, you may wish to forewarn the pastor that he might be prepared for this. Most pastors have at times had to remind everyone at the wedding rehearsal that the arrangements have been thought through, and the bride and groom have selected and prepared the ceremony as they would prefer. He then goes ahead with the rehearsal!

Making the Ceremony Unique

As you think about your wedding ceremony and plan for that special day, what an incredible opportunity exists to glorify the Lord, and create a memory that will be cherished throughout your lifetime! To make your wedding ceremony truly unique, add to it any of these special features.

The following special features will focus on three areas of the wedding ceremony. First, what can take place in the moments just before the wedding ceremony begins? Second, think about the processional. How will the bridal party enter the service? Third, what are the typical as well as unique features that can be added to the ceremony to make it truly spiritual?

The Moments Just Before the Wedding Ceremony Begins

Traditionally, the wedding ceremony begins with the seating of the bride's mother. This is a special moment in the service signifying the bride is ready, and the ceremony begins. Several very special features are possible during these moments.

Music

The bride, wedding coordinator, and minister work through the arrangement of the music selected to begin the service. The organist can offer good suggestions if the bridal couple so desires. In the final moments before the mother of the bride is seated, think of several musical possibilities.

1. A gifted family member quotes Song of Solomon 2:16, "My beloved is mine, and I am his," and sings a song dedicated to the couple.

2. If the bride or groom is gifted musically and if the church is equipped to pre-record the selection, the following reading could be played, followed by special music.

> **(If the bride is to sing)** "Today marks a new beginning in my life as I give myself to become the wife of (Groom's name). The Lord has blessed my life and brought me to this very special moment. As you witness the promises we make and rejoice in the love we share, please remember it is all because of the grace and blessing of the Lord. To my beloved, in a few moments, I will become your wife. My heart is full of love for you. I cherish you and desire to be a godly wife." (Special music follows.)

> **(If the groom is to sing)** "Today marks a new beginning in my life as I give myself to become the husband of (Bride's name). I cannot begin to describe to you the joy I have in my heart at this moment. The Lord has answered my prayers and brought to me a precious partner in life. As you witness the promises we are about to make, please remember it is all because of the grace and blessing of the Lord. To my beloved, in a few moments, I will become your husband. I cherish you and desire to be a godly husband." (Special music follows.)

3. Congregational singing can be a fitting way to begin the ceremony. Hymns that speak of the majesty of Christ as well as the Christian home and family create the atmosphere of genuine worship as well as celebration.

4. Occasionally a gifted family member or friend is able to write lyrics to be sung to tunes that are under public domain. This offers a special and creative way to begin the service. It is important to be sure the music is no longer under copyright. Generally, public domain includes music written before 1922. Various web sites offer public domain titles to be considered.

The lighting of the candles

Many weddings feature the unity candle during the ceremony. Three candles are displayed. Before the ceremony begins, the two outside candles are lit which represent the bride and groom. Typically the ushers light the candles. Here are several ways to creatively make this special, just before the wedding begins.

1. Both the mother of the bride and the mother of the groom walk together to the unity candles and light the outside candle representing their child.

2. The bride's parents and the groom's parents both come to the unity candle to light the outside candle representing their child. Following the lighting of the candle, a very special moment would occur if both fathers offered prayer for the Lord's blessing upon the new home and family to be established. Or the father of the bride may offer a prayer of thanksgiving for the son-in-law the Lord is bringing into his home and asks the Lord's blessing upon him. The father of the groom likewise offers a prayer of thanksgiving for the daughter-in-law the Lord is bring into his home and asks the Lord's blessing upon her. The father of the bride then joins the wedding processional to escort his daughter.

3. Another possibility is to involve the grandparents in someway in the lighting of the unity candle. As the candles are being lit, the grandparents stand and someone reads the following. "Today the generations of two homes stand as a tribute and testimony of the faithfulness of God and devotion of families. (Name of groom and name of bride) come together at this moment, to celebrate the amazing plan of God, and want you to know that they delight in your presence. A new home is established today as another generation embarks on the journey of a lifetime."

Readings

As the two candles at the unity candle display are lit, a precious moment exists to make the ceremony truly unique. A person who has played a special part in the life of either the bride or groom may be invited to share in the wedding ceremony at this point. Consider these special readings.

Special reading-"The Faithfulness of God"

"We are traveling on a journey along a road of many twists, turns, hills, and valleys. This journey of a lifetime begins at the moment of conception when a tiny little person comes into existence as an incredible result of the design of our creator God. These families have witnessed the birth, growth, and maturing of two individuals. The bride grew up in (location) and the groom grew up in (location). In a wonderful way, the Lord God has worked in their lives. (At this point, the reader will share how the couple met and one or two specifics as to how the Lord has worked in bringing them together.) Now we come to celebrate the faithfulness of God. Jeremiah the prophet declared with assurance in Lamentations 3:22-23, '...His compassions fail not. They are new every morning: great is thy faithfulness.' Truly God is faithful and may His blessing be upon (names of bride and groom)."

Special reading- "A Parent's Prayer"

This reading can be offered by one of the parents or shared by both the parents of the bride and parents of the groom.

"Many thoughts go through my mind, dear Lord, as I think back on the years I have had with my child. I remember the day we discovered a child would be coming to our home. Thoughts of joy were mixed with the sense of the responsibility of parenting. Then I held this child in my arms. I watched my little one fall asleep as I cradled (name of child) not only in my arms; but close to my heart. I experienced the overwhelming sense of love and awe as well as the desire to protect, and sheer wonder of being a parent. How amazingly fast the years have flown by! The first steps, the first days of kindergarten, the first bicycle ride seem like yesterday.

Here we are today. My child will become a life partner, married to another. My family grows in extension today as I welcome into my home and heart, the beloved of my child. May the days ahead be filled with love and devotion to you and to each other. May Christ be the head of this new home, and may the wonderful grace and peace of the Lord be part of their lives every day. Lord, may both (name of bride and groom) seek your will, find delight in serving you, and know the joy that comes in love that grows. May their love grow deeper as they travel on this journey of a lifetime. I ask this of You, dear Lord."

Special reading- "The Journey of Our Lives"

> Consider the possibility of asking an older individual or couple, to write in their own words the blessings experienced in their marriage. This can be a wonderful time when a couple married for many years very briefly writes of how God has met their needs, blessed their lives, and sustained them through the good as well as hard times. This provides a beautiful way for the ceremony to begin.

Special reading- "A Word from the Groom- The Prayer of My Heart"

A creative way to begin the wedding ceremony is to have the groom speak to the congregation immediately after the lighting of the two outside candles at the unity candle display. He may wish to write his own welcome and expression of joy. If he is not a writer, he may wish to read this note entitled "The Prayer of My Heart."

> "I want to welcome you as family and friends to share in our lives and celebrate our love. (Name of bride) and I want to thank you for coming. I also want you to know that as (Bride's name) husband, I sense deeply the responsibility of loving her as Christ loved the church. Before this ceremony begins, as the spiritual leader of our new home, I am asking the Lord to continue to work in our lives. It is the prayer of my heart that Christ would mold me into his image and to help me to become more like Him. It is the prayer of my heart that the Lord would help me to be strong of conviction, gentle in compassion, great in courage and godly in character. May His hand bless our home. May His Word guide our hearts. May His love fill our marriage and help us overcome every obstacle. May His wisdom lead us in each decision. Like Joshua of old, it is the prayer of my heart that as for me and my house, we will serve the Lord.
>
> This is the prayer of my heart for the glory of the Lord Jesus and the good of my beloved (Bride's name). Welcome to our wedding."

Special Features for the Processional

The typical and traditional processional has the bridal maids, the maid or matron of honor, the ring bearer and flower girl, followed by the father escorting his daughter into the ceremony. As the minister, groom and his groomsmen come into the auditorium, the processional begins and is completed with the father and the bride joining the rest of the party at the front of the church. There are several creative possibilities for the bridal couple to consider.

Groomsmen and bridesmaids meet

Before the arrival of the ring bearer and flower girl, a creative processional has the maids stopping in the aisle at approximately the halfway point. The corresponding groomsmen then walks down the aisle, meets the maid, turns and escorts her the rest of the way down the aisle. The groom also meets his bride in the aisle, shakes hands with the father, escorts his bride to the front with the father of the bride following closely and standing with the couple at the beginning of the ceremony.

Groom and bride only meet in the aisle

Some couples will prefer to have just the bride and groom meet for special escort. The father and bride stop in the aisle and wait for the groom to meet them. Shaking the groom's hand, the father gives his daughter to the groom, who escorts her to the front of the church. The father follows and stands with the wedding party awaiting his speaking part in the service.

Placement of the wedding party in the processional

The typical arrangement of the wedding party places them with their back to the congregation as they face the minister. Usually the wedding party is arranged in the following way.

Back of the Church Auditorium

Ring Bearer   Flower Girl

Groomsmen Best Man Groom Father Bride Maid/Matron Maids

Minister

Front of the Church Auditorium

A special feature that some bridal couples appreciate has the same basic arrangement, except for the direction they face. In this special feature, the bridal party comes to their assigned spot in the front of the church. Following the father of the bride giving his daughter to be married, the bridal party will turn toward the congregation. As the entire party faces the assembled guests, the minister takes his place in the front center, facing the bridal party with his back to the congregation.

Special Features for the Wedding Ceremony

The possibilities are nearly unlimited in creating a unique and special ceremony. Typical special features include special music, Scripture readings and the lighting of the unity candle from the two outside candles. The officiating pastor may wish to offer some of the additional special features that can be placed in the wedding ceremony at the pleasure of the pastor and bridal couple, in addition to these ideas.

Special honor to the parents of the bride and groom

Some bridal couples wish to honor their parents in the wedding ceremony by presenting a special gift. The bride gives the gift to her parents as the groom gives a gift to his parents. Typically the parents are not told about this so as to be surprised in the service. A variation of this act would be to reverse the giving of the gifts. Here the bride would come to her husband's parents and the groom to his bride's parents. This is a tender expression of love and appreciation to the parents.

Special tribute to the Lord for His wonderful leading

This tribute provides a tender moment in the service and makes it truly unique to the couple. The officiating pastor with the help of the bridal couple fills in the blanks and reads the following tribute.

> Proverbs 3:5-6 says, "Trust in the Lord with all thine heart, and lean not unto thine own understanding. In all thy ways acknowledge him, and he shall direct thy paths." Today, we as family and friends gather to recognize and celebrate the incredible way the Lord has directed the paths of (name of Groom) and (name of Bride).

(Groom) was born in (name of town). As a child he grew up in (name of town and state). He placed his trust in the Lord Jesus as Savior at the age of (age). God tenderly worked in his life. (Bride) was born in (name of town and state). As a child she grew up in (name of town and state). She placed her trust in the Lord Jesus as Savior at the age of (age). God tenderly worked in her life.

"And He shall direct thy paths," so says the Lord. In a special way, the Lord has directed in the lives of (Groom) and (Bride). They met (testimony of how they met and how the Lord has directed them to this day. This may include a humorous event, special direction in their lives, or whatever their testimony might be).

We as their family and friends give thanks to the Lord for the way He has directed their paths. There is no improvement on the will of God. Though the road will not be easy, great is the joy of knowing the Lord's direction and trusting Him for the days ahead.

Special charge to the couple

The officiating pastor or invited special guest may share the following charge to the couple. This is a great opportunity to invest both in the couple to be married as well as in the marriages of the invited guests.

Today marks the day of a new beginning. We gather here as your family and friends to share the joy of this moment and to witness the sacred vows you share today. The uniting of your lives and the establishing of your new home is special not only to us; but is special to the Lord Himself. It is my privilege to present to you a solemn but also joyful charge. A charge is that by which one is reminded and entrusted with the sacred responsibility assigned to him or her. (Groom) and (Bride), as you stand before the Lord and these witnesses, I charge you today to honor the Lord your God in all your ways.

(Groom), as the head of this new home and the spiritual leader of your family, I charge to love your wife as Christ loved His church. I charge you to be a devoted, faithful, loving, protecting and godly husband. I charge you to keep yourself from any temptation that would hurt your marriage. May the enabling of the Lord and the empowering of His Word be yours everyday.

(Bride), as the partner and wife of (Groom), I charge you to follow the Lord your God and to be all He wants you to be. I charge you to encourage your husband. Be a devoted, faithful, loving, and godly wife. I charge you to be gracious in your actions and devoted in your commitment to your husband. I charge you to be a woman of prayer and godly character. I charge you to keep yourself from any temptation that would hurt your marriage. May God enable you to follow Him every day.

Special reading-"When Two People Really Love"

We read of Isaac's love for Rebekah his bride. Genesis 24:67 states, "And Isaac brought her into his mother's tent, and took Rebekah, and she became his wife; and he loved her." Isaac grew up in a home that honored the Lord. He saw the Lord's blessing upon his parents and their walk with God. But something was missing in his life. In a wonderful way, the Lord incredibly brought to him Rebekah, his beloved. And he loved her.

When two people come together at the leading of the Lord, a wonderful relationship of love is established. This love grows deep as it is centered in the Lord. When two people really love each other, they will discover encouragement in discouraging days. They will receive grace in times that are stressful. They will find forgiveness in the moments when misunderstandings happen. When two people really love each other, there is no obstacle too big to overcome. There is no trial too hard to endure. There is no hardship too heavy to bear.

When two people really love each other, a home of godliness is established. A closeness of fellowship is experienced and an intimacy is realized that is more precious than all the gold of the mines, and more valuable than all the wealth of Wall Street. When two people really love each other, it really is as long as life shall last. This love comes from the One who loves you both more than anyone else could ever love you. This love that lasts a lifetime is from the Lord Jesus who loves you with all of His heart.

Special Scripture passages

A wedding ceremony offers the special opportunity of planting seeds in the lives of the family and friends invited. Couples may wish to have

Scripture inserted in their ceremony. Among the many passages of Scripture that could be used, here is a partial list of possibilities.

- Genesis 2:18-25
- Genesis 24:61-67
- Psalm 8
- Psalm 16:5-11
- Psalm 33:1-5
- Psalm 100
- Psalm 127

- Psalm 128
- 1 Corinthians 13
- Ephesians 5:21-33
- Colossians 1:9-18
- Titus 2:1-8, 11-13
- 1 Peter 3:1-12

Special presentation of the bride and groom

Traditionally the father of the bride is asked, "Who gives this woman to be married to this man?" He usually answers, "Her mother and I do."

A special feature that makes the wedding ceremony unique is the creative way the couple is given and presented to each other. In this feature, when asked, "Who gives this woman to be married to this man?" The mother of the bride joins the wedding party, and states with her husband, "**We joyfully give our daughter.**" (Mother and father of the bride then kiss daughter, shakes the hand of the groom or hug him and are seated.) The minister then asks, "Who gives this man to be married to this woman?" His parents come, and take their place with the groom and state, "**We joyfully give our son.**" (His parents then hug him and hug the bride as well.)

The officiating pastor then says, "How beautifully from two different families, one new family forms today. As parents, your greatest joy comes from seeing your children walk in truth. May the home established today be a home of joy, and truth built upon the solid foundation of Christ."

Special reading-"A Parent's Prayer"

This reading could be read by either set of parents or a parent from both sets.

> Lord, today is an amazing day. It is a day that I imagined long ago and it has arrived much faster than I ever dreamed. Lord, our children come before You today to share their joy and promise each other their lives.

Lord, as this day has come, we the parents of (Groom) and (Bride) are filled with wonder and awe at your precious leading. I pray for our children today. I pray for their home that it will be a shining tribute of You and Your grace. I pray for their marriage. May it be a union that is marked by kindness, forgiveness, joy, and love. I pray today that their joy would be full and their blessings many.

Lord, I do not pray that You would make them rich. I pray You would supply their need. Lord, I do not pray You would make the way easy. I pray You would direct their steps. Lord, I do not pray You would make them famous. I pray You would give them good friends that would encourage, and enrich them with a friendship centered in You.

Lord, today has come and with it our heartfelt thanks, as parents who love You and pray the very best for our children.

Special reading-"A Marriage Built On Christ"

Wise couples trust the Lord and daily understand.

We're here by His good leading and secure in His precious hand.

Together we enter our marriage. I will love you all of my life.

May this sacred union be blessed, as a godly husband and wife.

We truly need the Lord's blessing in all we say and do.

By His grace, and help each day my love, I promise to be true.

The words of our vows, our covenant will last throughout our life.

I rejoice in this special moment when we become husband and wife.

Before this assembly we promise, to follow the Lord everyday.

May He give power and blessing and guard the words we say.

May we quickly be forgiving when those hurts surely come.

May our home be Christ-like always, and our hearts to Him belong.

Dismissal of the Wedding Guests

Traditionally, the bridal party participates in the recessional following the presentation and introduction of the new married couple. The wedding party assembles in a line in the foyer as the designated groomsman returns to escort the bride's parents first and then the second groomsman escorts the groom's parents to the receiving line. Two groomsmen return to dismiss the assembly row by row beginning with the bride's side.

Some bridal couples prefer to dismiss the congregation personally by returning to the front of the auditorium. Together they dismiss row by row, briefly greeting family and friends in the aisle. This provides a precious moment to share the joy and dismiss the assembly often more quickly. Guests are not as apt to stand and speak at length in the aisle in front of other guests as they will in the foyer! It is a nice way to greet and proceed to pictures and the reception.

The possibilities are nearly unlimited in creating and fashioning a truly unique and biblical wedding. May your joy be full as your work with your pastor-counselor who dearly loves you and desires God's best for you.

A Time of Celebration

This is an outstanding opportunity for you to understand that the reception is the first official act in your newly married lives. As believers, we are to live new, Christ-changed lives (2 Corinthians 5:17). The wedding reception of two redeemed people who love the Lord Jesus should be very different from the reception of two unsaved people from the world!

Your reception provides a wonderful opportunity for fun and fellowship. Precious possibilities to make a truly creative and unique reception are available to you as a couple. Therefore, there are several questions you and your fiancé must consider:

1. Does our reception glorify the Lord Jesus and give Him a preeminent place?
2. Does our reception abstain from anything that is of the world and contrary to sound doctrine?
3. Does our reception clearly present the blessing and joy of a biblical home and family to those attending?
4. Does our reception celebrate the goodness of the Lord in bringing us as a couple together?
5. Does our reception establish the permanence of pledging our love for our lifetime as a couple?
6. Does our reception create a day that will bring memories of joy throughout the years to come?
7. Does our reception provide opportunity for the families to clearly see the establishment of a new home and biblical family?
8. Does our reception focus on the establishment of marriage as being God's plan and His idea?
9. Does our reception enhance and elevate the marriage of believers and the joy which comes from the Lord?

Creative Ideas for Godly Receptions

As a believing couple, make your reception truly different. Here are several suggestions to consider.

Forget a modified "Christian" toast

Raising glasses, and pretending the sparkling grape juice is champagne should be meaningless to a godly believer. Rather, bring both sets of parents as well as the bride and groom for a special presentation and prayer. Consider having the groom's parents stand beside the bride, and the bride's parents stand beside the groom. A special prayer asking the Lord to bless the couple is a great testimony.

A brief statement of testimony

The best man and/or the matron or maid of honor sharing a testimony would be a great memory maker for the guests. This could be a time of sharing how the Lord brought the bride and groom together, or it could be a time of sharing how God has blessed their individual lives through the friendship of the bride, and groom. It may also include a testimony of how the bride and groom came to personal faith in the Lord Jesus Christ.

Special readings

Any of the readings offered in the wedding ceremony could easily be incorporated into the reception activities.

Brief Power Point presentation

If given enough time to prepare, a wonderful possibility exists in the production of a Power Point presentation of the bride and groom. This would include photos from infancy up to the present. A note of caution would concern the length of the presentation. Neither the bride nor groom will desire a lengthy slide show!

Special music

As in the wedding ceremony, special music in the reception can be a huge blessing. Other couples may enjoy quiet music in the background during the time of eating at the reception.

Gifts

Many couples appreciate the opportunity of returning home to a much smaller circle of family to open the gifts. If this is possible, often it is much more enjoyable. Several should be asked ahead of time to collect the gifts. These should be stored at the home of trusted family or friends, not in the empty apartment of the honeymooning couple.

While this volume does not address the honeymoon, excellent resources are available for the couple to read and use. See Chapter Six for several suggestions.

Countdown to the Wedding

This is a suggested time line for basic wedding schedules. Detailed wedding planners are abundant. Some will offer a more basic plan, while others are much more detailed for weddings that are large and somewhat extravagant.

Once you are engaged

1. Begin to think through the wedding budget. This will determine the size and style of the wedding. As the bride, you must talk with your parents and decide who will pay for specific details of the wedding. The next chapter will offer a suggestion as to who pays for the various details of the wedding and reception. Determine that the Lord will be glorified throughout the wedding and the reception. This is a time to glorify Him, not glamorize yourselves.

2. Select a wedding date and time. Speak with your pastor and book the church and fellowship hall for the reception.

3. Will you be using a wedding coordinator? Work with your pastor in the selection of the wedding coordinator as well as the exact expectations you have concerning her role.

4. Ask the pastor his procedure and dates for premarital counseling. Assure him you are eager to prepare for your marriage. Determine to be on guard. Do not allow temptation to cause you to experience moral impurity.

5. Register at local bridal registries. Target, Wal-Mart, Bed Bath and Beyond, and JC Penny are but a few of such stores.

6. Select and retain the photographer. Be sure to compare prices, and what the photographer offers in the package. Wise stewardship really demands careful selection of each venue of your wedding and reception.

Six months before the wedding ceremony

1. Begin to compile the guest list. A great source for the various family members and friends will come from both moms. What about the church family? Begin to discuss how they will be invited. Will a general announcement of invitation be made with a sign-up sheet? Or will individuals within the church family receive specific invitation?

2. Select and order the wedding gown. Make sure there is plenty of time for it to arrive and any alterations to take place. This is the special day for the bride. However, as a godly believer you must be sure the gown passes the following tests. (1) The modesty test-is any thing showing that should not be? (2) The stewardship test-while it is for a very special occasion, the average length of time a bride wears her gown is less than four hours. Is the amount of money this specific bridal gown costs a wise investment? When a four hour gown costs the same as four months rent, is this really wise? (3) The comfort test-is this comfortable and will you enjoy being in this for the hours of the ceremony, pictures and reception?

3. Double-check with the pastor as to when he wishes to begin premarital counseling. Probably at this point, the pastor will wish to schedule your first appointment. Do not be surprised if he has several pages of information for you to fill out and submit before your first appointment.

4. Work with your wedding coordinator in retaining the services of the organist, janitor, videographer, florist, and double-check with the photographer to make sure the date is still confirmed.

5. Some bridal couples send out a "Be sure to save the date card" for our wedding.

6. Choose the wedding rings.

7. Send the engagement announcements to the newspapers.

8. Select the attendants (bridesmaids and groomsmen). These should be people who are either related to the bridal couple or who are really significant in the friendship. In a truly godly wedding, the attendants should be like minded believers who are walking with the Lord.

9. Select the wedding cake. Wise shopping will really pay off in the cake selection. Will the cake come from a professional bakery, or will it be made by a friend or acquaintance?

10. Complete the honeymoon plans. If you are traveling outside the country, check on visa, passports and any required inoculations.
11. Check on the availability and prices of salons if the bride and her maids will require their services.
12. Book the caterer and enter the contractual agreement to reserve the date. This can only be completed after the couple decides what kind of reception they will have. Will it be a cake and punch reception? Will it be a sit-down catered meal? Who will be paying for it? What is affordable?
13. Check with area motels. If possible to hold a block of rooms without penalty for cancellation, it will be wise to do so.

Four months before the wedding ceremony

1. Confirm the final details with the caterer, and double-check the date to be sure it is confirmed. A written contract should be signed by both the caterer and the person who is paying for the reception.
2. Order and purchase items not being furnished by the caterer for the reception and ceremony. Wedding receptions are negotiable as to what the caterer will include in the price. Decide carefully what the family will furnish, and what will be part of the caterer's price.
3. Order the wedding invitations.
4. Visit with the photographer to work out specific details of the wedding and reception.
5. Check with the florist to confirm your wishes for the flowers. You will most likely have to at least make a partial payment, if not pay in full at this time.
6. Begin to gather estimates for the decorations for the reception.
7. Purchase the wedding rings.
8. Order tuxedos for the groomsmen and the fathers.
9. Check with the local city or village clerk as to marriage license requirements.

Two months before the wedding ceremony

1. Meet with your wedding coordinator to review details and deadlines for the wedding and reception.
2. Mail invitations to the invited guests. This is usually done between six weeks and two months before the wedding.

3. Finalize arrangements for out-of-town attendants and guests. Where will they stay? By this time, there are so many details to work through, it is often much easier for out-of-town guests to be furnished the name of the motel or motels available, along with the telephone numbers. Make it clear that the bridal couple and families would really appreciate their booking their own rooms.
4. Select a small but meaningful gift for the attendants and those helping with the wedding.
5. Check with the Social Security Administration concerning the bride's name change and her social security number.
6. The couple will be scheduling regular counseling appointments with the pastor. Commit to taking seriously the tests, assignments and counsel provided by your pastor. You will want to demonstrate your appreciation to him.

One month before the wedding ceremony
1. Meet regularly with the wedding coordinator. Check, double-check, and review the details on the wedding coordinator's list.
2. Double-check with all vendors to make sure the date is confirmed.
3. Have final fitting for bridal party.
4. Have groomsmen fitted for tuxedos.
5. Check with newspaper on wedding announcement requirements.
6. Finalize plans with the pastor as well as finalize plans for the rehearsal dinner.

These are merely suggested time tables. Some couples wish to work on some of the items a little earlier than the suggested time frame. It is fine to work earlier; but not wise to wait until later than the suggested dates.

List other items to be checked on that are not listed in this chapter.

_____

_____

_____

_____

_____

I cannot finish everything in simply one lone day.

So, Lord, help me to get organized, and trust You on the way.

This all is very new to me; I've never been this way before.

So please give me understanding as I seek You more and more.

Who Pays for What in the Wedding and Reception?

How do you know who usually pays for the various items in the wedding and reception? There are no set hard-and-fast rules for who pays for what in the upcoming ceremony. Several circumstances contribute to the question of funding. Are you as the couple employed with adequate salaries, and will you have a significant part in paying for the wedding or reception? On the other hand, will the parents of the bride be paying significantly for this wonderful event?

While there are no absolutes, typically the following individuals pay for the various items in the wedding ceremony.

The bride typically pays for the following:
- The wedding ring for the groom
- Gifts for her attendants
- A small gift for her husband (if they choose to give each other a gift)
- A bridesmaid's luncheon (if one is planned)
- Wedding night lingerie and items to be taken on the honeymoon

The groom typically pays for the following:
- The wedding ring for the bride
- Honeymoon vacation
- Wedding gift for the bride (if they choose to give each other a gift)
- Gifts for the groomsmen
- Pastor's honorarium

The bride's family typically pays for the following:
- The wedding ceremony costs
- The bride's attire
- The wedding invitations, announcements, thank-you notes
- The wedding photographer
- The wedding organist and church janitor
- The florist
- The reception

  Note: Many parents find it helpful and encouraging to give the bridal couple a set amount of money to be used for the wedding ceremony and reception. Whatever the couple does not use is theirs for whatever expenses they have (rent, etc.)

The groom's family typically pays for the following:
- Their attire and the rehearsal dinner

The attendants typically pay for the following:
- The attire to be worn in the wedding
- Gifts to be given to the newlyweds
- Their own transportation to and from the wedding

Our Adjustments as a Couple Six Months Later

Many couples appreciate the sessions of premarital counseling in preparing them for married life. You and your pastor have invested many hours together. The greatest success of any type of counseling depends on the sincerity and commitment of the counselees in applying Scriptural directives and principles.

Work on this section before your counseling session

Now another great opportunity exists as you invest a little time with your pastor in following up in the first few months of your marriage. A special test entitled "Now That We Are Married" should be completed early enough to give your counselor plenty of time to prepare this session. Also, fill in section 10 once again now that you are married. Your counselor will be using the answers you gave before your wedding in Section 10 of the assignment "The Road Already Traveled." You will find it interesting to see how your answers compare now with the answers completed before your wedding.

Now That We Are Married

Name _____

List three things for which you are thankful in your marriage: _____

_____

_____

List three things you appreciate about your mate: _____

_____

.

_____

Use a scale of 1 to 5 to answer the following questions.
   1= Very dissatisfied and very concerned, needs immediate attention
   2= Dissatisfied and concerned, we need to work on this
   3= All right, but surely could improve
   4= Satisfied with this situation and appreciate this blessing
   5= Very satisfied and thank the Lord for this and will not take it for
   granted

Mark the appropriate number by circling it for your answer. Place an X
over the number you believe will be your partner's level of satisfaction.
Please do not work on this together. Work separately and prayerfully on
your answers.

   1. The state of our walk with the Lord as a couple   1 2 3 4 5

   2. The routine we are developing in reading the Bible and praying to-
      gether 1 2 3 4 5

   3. Our involvement in our local church   1 2 3 4 5

   4. The daily time invested in talking with each other   1 2 3 4 5

   5. The quality of free time we have to spend with each on a regular basis
      1 2 3 4 5

   6. The amount of time we are apart from each other because of work
      and other activities 1 2 3 4 5

   7. The way we are managing our money 1 2 3 4 5

   8. The way we are adjusting to each other   1 2 3 4 5

   9. The way we are making decisions together 1 2 3 4 5

   10. The way we are managing conflicts when differing opinions surface
      1 2 3 4 5

11. Our sexual interaction with each other 1 2 3 4 5

12. Our level of involvement with friends and doing things with other couples 1 2 3 4 5

13. My spouse's relationship with my parents 1 2 3 4 5

14. My relationship with my spouse's parents 1 2 3 4 5

15. The level of satisfaction with our marriage 1 2 3 4 5

What are some of the situations you wish to discuss with the pastor?

_____

_____

_____

The Road Already Traveled- Section 10

Section 10. Complete the following statements in your own words.

A. When I think about marriage, I feel- _____

_____

_____

_____

B. Some of the things I appreciate about my mate include- _____

_____

_____

_____

C. Among my expectations in marriage, several that are very important to me include- _____

_____

_____

_____

D. Several areas that need to improve in my life would include- _____

_____

_____

_____

Several areas that need to improve in the life of my mate would include-

_____

_____

_____

E. When I think of the number of children I would like to have it would be-

_____

_____

_____

F. When I think of the ideal way of spending an evening together with my mate, it would be- _____

_____

_____

_____

G. When I think of the ideal vacation, it would be- _____

_____

_____

_____

Make arrangements with the pastor to make copies of these assignments. Be sure to submit them to him in plenty of time for him to prepare for this follow up counseling session.

Work on this section during your counseling session

During the dating, courtship, engagement, and days of premarital counseling, many couples are on guard and demonstrate their very best behavior with each other. Some couples soon slip into the routine and "busyness" of life, and before they know it, a dangerous situation of taking each other for granted can begin to form.

Be determined that no matter how busy life becomes, no matter how many things clamor for your attention, by the grace of God, you shall not take each other and your marriage for granted. Think carefully through these principles and safeguard your marriage to keep it in the highest priority and freshness. Be ready to continue to embrace these commitments.

Commitment to _____

Matthew 6:19-21 warns against being focused on treasure that is "here and now" in nature. Rather, be rich in laying up treasure in Heaven. This speaks about keeping spiritual, and eternal things in high priority. Then the Lord Jesus makes the application by saying, "For where your treasure is, there will your heart be also" (verse 21). Are your hearts as the married couple truly focused on the spiritual aspects of a successful marriage? Do your lives demonstrate that you have wholeheartedly committed to working on the growth and maturity of your relationship?

Investment in marriage requires time, talking, and truthfulness with yourself and each other. Are you as husband and wife clearly growing in your relationship? Are your hearts really into your marriage and making it work?

Are you really committed to being sensitive and understanding with each other? Paul's writing to the Colossian believers in 3:12-13 provides a list of characteristics the Lord desires to grow, and display in every believer, regardless of temperament, and personality. Understanding these concepts provides rich blessings in marriages and families.

1. Bowels of mercies (12a) has to do with a heart of compassion. It is the opposite of being harsh, cruel, mean spirited, or obnoxious. This heart of compassion should overflow with care for the other person.

2. Kindness (12b) is a thoughtful demonstration toward the other, a sweetness of attitude and action. This will be seen in the details of sharing household chores, encouraging each other, and the quality of time spent together.

3. Humbleness of mind and meekness (12c) does not act as a doormat willingly to be walked all over by another individual. Rather, it is the gentleness and graciousness extended to others. It is the opposite of being arrogant and haughty.

4. Longsuffering (12d) will be expressed with patience even if you have been provoked. It is the opposite of being short-fused and explosive when things do not go the way you wish. Steadfastness and perseverance are both essential elements of possessing longsuffering.

5. Forbearing one another (13a) is much more than just putting up with people. This concept expressed by Paul to the Colossian believers demonstrates sustaining, enduring, and bearing with people. It extends grace where grace is not merited. Truth is communicated with carefulness and loving tenderness. When there is a disagreement, confrontation is not explosive but quiet and timely.

6. Forgiving one another (13b) cancels the debt of the offender. It is the response of the wounded party when the guilty person apologizes and asks to be forgiven. Genuine forgiveness does not keep a score card of wounds to bring up later. Forgiveness is granted on the basis of how Christ has freely forgiven us.

These essential elements are the consistent and typical actions of a marriage that is adjusting well to each other and working through areas of potential conflict.

Additional Notes from this Counseling Session

_____

_____

_____

_____

Commitment to _____

The writer of Hebrews points out three serious roots of sin from which a wide variety of sinful actions will grow. From these three roots, sins of omission as well as sins of commission originate.

1. Root of bitterness (Hebrews 12:15a). This bitterness is an anger and resentment that is just below the surface. While everyone experiences times of anger, this is beyond the typical. This is an angry person, who allows bitterness to grow and fester.

   Several of the outflows of the angry person include seeking revenge, wrath, loss of temper, slamming doors, screaming, words of venom, a mean spirit as well as grumbling and complaining about how unfair things are. Anger is like a cancerous growth that, if left untreated not only destroys healthy bodies, but it brings about devastation in relationships.

   Do you or your spouse display resentment or anger? Your pastor will greatly desire to help you both to be overcomers if you will be honest with him. Do not pretend a problem does not exist. Be honest with yourself, your mate, and your pastor if there is an anger issue.

2. Fornication (12:16a). From this word, _pornos_ comes the wide range of illicit and sinful sexual activities. God has created a beautiful expression of intense intimacy for the husband and wife in the warmth of emotional intimacy and the act of sexual intercourse. The enemy of home and marriage has defiled this expression with sordid temptation and opportunity to lust. Pornography and unfaithfulness are great enemies of the home, and family.

Counseling in the realm of sexual matters frequently is uncomfortable for both for you as the couple as well as for the pastor. However, a healthy sexual relationship and growth in emotional intimacy are very important elements in a healthy marriage. Sex and intimacy are two different things. Both are necessary for a healthy marriage. What areas of protection are built into your marriage? As relating to internet, what type of filter do you have? Is your computer out in the open where secrecy is not typical? How much quality free time do you as the couple have on a weekly basis? Are there areas through which you and your mate must be counseled in this area?

3. Profane living (12:16b). Here the idea of profanity is presented in the words that are communicated and lifestyle that is lived. Literally this profanity pictures a person coming to the threshold of the door and being denied entrance because of a violation or making common what God says is holy. It is demonstrated by wrong values, self-focus, and wrong priorities. The attitudes of self-gratification (I want it now), self-indulgence (I have a right to be happy), and self-interest (I am the most important person in the whole wide world) express themselves through attitudes and choices of the heart.

Wrong values, jealousy, covetousness, poor money management, worldly living, and dishonesty are several of the ways this enemy of the home is manifested. One of the most dangerous situations a newly established home faces is the accumulation of debt to accumulate possessions. Unwise couples insist upon having things right now that took many years of working and saving for their parents to acquire. Indebtedness is a web woven that is difficult to break through.

Additional Notes from this Counseling Session

_____

_____

_____

_____

The postwedding follow-up counseling session will be helpful only to the extent that both the husband and the wife are honest with each other and their pastor. If there is a situation with which you need help in your adjustment, do not allow this opportunity to pass. This can be time well invested for you, as the couple, as you begin your lifetime together.

As your counseling session concludes, think about these principles for continuing to build a strong marriage. Implement them consistently, tenderly, and with great affection. You really can have a strong marriage. However, please remember that it will not happen automatically.

Fifteen Ways to Build a Strong Marriage

Marriages, in some ways, are similar to building a house. Both must be built on strong foundations, directions must be followed, and careful attention to details must be given. Developing a daily consistency in the following areas will help you to build a strong marriage. It is well worth the time and investment.

1. Be sure you and your mate are becoming best friends.
2. Develop good conversational skills. Do not interrupt. Look at each other. Speak clearly without sarcasm or hurtful words.
3. Share openly with each other about your fears, concerns and what you are thinking.
4. Learn to be considerate of your mate's feelings.
5. Develop the skill to become better aware of the little details of life and the home, which will demonstrate thoughtfulness to your mate.
6. Avoid developing a critical spirit. Do not criticize your mate. When you must address a situation, express it carefully, prayerfully and tenderly.
7. Frequently tell your mate of your love.
8. Become good in demonstrating that you are not taking your mate for granted.
9. Never be in competition with your mate.
10. Discover God's purpose for your life.
11. Determine to grow as a Christian.
12. Find ways to serve the Lord together.

13. Ask the Lord to help you to reach an agreement concerning earning, savings, investing, spending and sharing your money.
14. Respect your mate.
15. Work at having a great relationship with the extended family. However always remember, your first priority is the Lord and next to your mate.

"Together- What a Beautiful Word"

Together we've walked with the Lord hand in hand,

Our marriage is built on the rock, not sifting sand.

It has sometimes been hard; but always we've known,

Always be careful. We will reap what we've sown.

So we've sown kindness and joy, and of course lots of love.

Our blessings are many, He has showered from above.

We're convinced as we travel, God's will is the best,

Seek Him first and we'll find, He'll supply all the rest.

Matthew 6:33, "Seek ye first the kingdom of God and His righteousness, and all these things shall be added unto you."

Make the Lord the center of your marriage. Build your lives upon His Word. Seek His wisdom and blessing on a daily basis. You really can have a great marriage on your journey of a lifetime.

www.ingramcontent.com/pod-product-compliance
Lightning Source LLC
Chambersburg PA
CBHW060945040426
42445CB00011B/1011